AF316702

Courting Athena

Courting Athena

A Short Introduction to Philosophy

Zach Lee

WIPF & STOCK · Eugene, Oregon

COURTING ATHENA
A Short Introduction to Philosophy

Wipf & Stock
An Imprint of Wipf and Stock Publishers
199 W. 8th Ave., Suite 3
Eugene, OR 97401

www.wipfandstock.com

PAPERBACK ISBN: 979-8-3852-0036-8
HARDCOVER ISBN: 979-8-3852-0037-5
EBOOK ISBN: 979-8-3852-0038-2

VERSION NUMBER 101023

Contents

What Is Philosophy?

A FEW YEARS AGO, I saw a meme about philosophy.

The meme pictured a man lying on the ground and clutching his chest due to a heart attack. A crying woman hunched over his fallen body and, in tears, looked up and screamed, "Help! We need a doctor." A smug-looking man wearing a suit quickly ran up and said, "I'm a doctor . . . a doctor of philosophy." The woman pointed to the man who had the heart attack and said, "He's dying!," to which the doctor coolly and contemplatively replied, "We are all dying."

We are all philosophers

When one thinks of *philosophy*, many different images come to mind. For example, one may think of the doctor in this particular meme (who is so caught up with big ideas that he doesn't even notice a man having a heart attack). One may think of an ancient Greek peripatetic walking around the ancient columns in Athens with his arms crossed and holding his chin with one hand. One may think of a Hindu guru practicing meditation near the Ganges River with his eyes closed and legs crossed. One may think of a professor at a university wearing a tweed jacket with leather patches on the elbows saying something like "And ninthly! . . ." One may think of medieval clerics arguing over how many angels can dance on the head of a pin.[1] One may think of well-paid attorneys working for large legal firms using arguments to try to win high-profile cases in court. But there is a problem with all of these examples. Though they are accurate (every single one of them is technically an example of people doing philosophy), they don't reflect the primary way that philosophy is done. *Philosophy is something done by every single one of us every single day, whether we know it or not.*

Oftentimes we think that philosophy, whatever it is, relates to "head in the clouds" or "ivory tower" thinking. We assume that it is impractical, ethereal, and serves no purpose other than to play speculative mind games or to create logical quandaries. But, as we will see, nothing is more practical than philosophy. Since philosophy has to do with questions, answers, reasons, knowledge, and truth, we are all philosophers, and we are doing philosophy all the time.

When you consider yourself to be a religious person or nonreligious person, you are doing philosophy (philosophy of religion). When you think a certain action like committing sexual assault or using a racial slur is morally evil, you are doing philosophy (ethics). When you think that people should have the right to choose their political leaders by voting, you are doing philosophy (political philosophy). When you think that the dress you are wearing looks beautiful, you are doing philosophy (aesthetics). When you think that atoms make up larger objects, you are doing philosophy (philosophy of science). When you can easily find your car in a grocery store parking lot because you know what properties your car has—color, size, etc.—you are doing philosophy (metaphysics). When you interpret any text, including this very sentence that you are now reading, you are doing philosophy (philosophy of language). Even when you make a claim such as "I don't think I'm a philosopher," you are doing philosophy (logic). *There is no not doing philosophy. The question is not "Are we philosophers?" We all are. The question is "Will we be good ones?"*

What is philosophy?

Asking the question "What is philosophy?" is itself a very philosophical question. It doesn't have an easy answer. That is because philosophy is not like any other subject. Yes, the word *philosophy* means the "love of wisdom"—from the Greek words *phileō* (love) and *sophia* (wisdom)—but that only pushes the question back further. *What exactly is this mysterious "love of wisdom"?* In other subjects, such as physics, economics, medicine, or music, one has to stay within certain boundaries, use certain methods, and ask certain questions. Using a saxophone to try to create a rocket ship doesn't work very well, because these objects are in completely different fields. Trying to project who will win an election by studying the weight of light beams doesn't work very well, because the theories are in completely separate fields. But philosophy is not like that. Philosophy is not like any other specific, limited field of study. *Philosophy asks the questions behind the questions.*

Philosophy gets a say in every field of inquiry. In fact, for most of Western history, things such as science, sociology, psychology, physics, and aesthetics were not separate fields of study (as they are today). Rather, they were simply subcategories of philosophy (because philosophy studies every-thing). Philosophy is more like the skeleton within or the method behind every other field of inquiry. One cannot do a scientific experiment without asking things such as "What would count as solid proof of my hypothesis?" *This means that even when someone tries to prove something in a lab, they have begun with philosophical assumptions that were not proved in a lab.* This means that even when someone says something with which we all already agree (I at least hope you agree!) such as "Genocide is bad," they are doing philosophy and have and should have a reason for why they are saying what they are saying.

When a piece of music seems beautiful, philosophy asks: "What is beauty?" "Is beauty objective?" and "How do we know this particular piece of music is actually beautiful?" When science says that a new medicine works well, philosophy asks: "How do we know that it works well if it hasn't been tried for very long?" "Was the medicine's research conducted in an ethical way?" and "Does a patient have the right to refuse the medicine if the result is that they will die without it?" Philosophy is the craft that one has to practice (or at least take for granted) before they can discover anything else in any other field. *Philosophy is the ground on which other fields of inquiry stand.*

Some fields of study build the frame or the sheetrock or the roof of the house. Other fields put in the windows, paint the walls, and fix the plumb-ing. But philosophy is the house's foundation on which all those other areas of knowledge stand. If the foundation is off, the walls will be crooked. If the foundation is off, the windows will slant. If the foundation is off, the ceiling will begin to show cracks and nail holes. Whereas a scientist might claim that light travels 186,000 miles per second, a philosopher asks questions like: "What is light?" "Is light a substance?" "How do we know that the light we see is the same light that other people see?" "How do you know the light is not just made up by your mind?" "If everyone were blind, would we still know that light exits?" "Is light infinite?" "Does light travel at an absolute speed or relative speed?" or "Why do we still 'see' light when we are dreaming if the room we sleep in is completely dark?"

Philosophy is pushing the mind to its limits by trying to gain as much knowledge as we can in any sphere of inquiry. More precisely, philosophy is an attempt to know correct things in the areas of truth (logic), reality (metaphysics), knowledge (epistemology), religion (theology), ethics (morality), justice (politics), aesthetics (beauty), and in every other area. Philosophy asks the deepest questions and tries to come up with the most consistent answers to these mind-boggling inquiries. Philosophy is the study of reasoning. When you believe something, make a decision, or act (in any way whatsoever) you will find yourself attaching reasons to your belief, decision, or action. And every time you do this you are doing philosophy. Philosophy cares about what is true and being able to give a defense for why we know it is true.

Perhaps my favorite definition of philosophy comes from a lecture I once heard and the definition is attributed to David Hills at Stanford University: *"Philosophy is the art of asking questions that come naturally to children, using methods that come naturally to lawyers."* In this sense, philosophy asks the deepest and most basic questions we can ask and then tries to answer them by using a dialectic of rigorous argumentation.

What makes this book unique?

Why do we need another introduction to philosophy? After all, there are many that have been written by people much smarter than I. *My hope is that this introduction to philosophy will be as accessible and easy to understand as possible.* It is designed to take someone who is not very familiar with the subject and give them a helpful starting point into this incredible field. Though it could be used in an undergraduate philosophy class, the average adult should be able to pick it up and read it through without wanting to punch a wall or throw the book across the room in frustration.

Philosophy is one of the most difficult subjects to study. It is not for the faint of heart. It can be very abstract; it uses a lot of jargon; and it deals with very difficult topics (such as infinity, God, selfhood, immaterial objects, and political theory—to name just a few). I have never read a philosophy textbook that I thought really "held the reader's hand" through the process. Many introductions to philosophy are dry, sterile, and esoteric. This causes students to lose interest in what should be a thrilling study. Other introductions are just anthologies of some of the greatest thinkers in world history.[2]

Those are not bad, per se, but for someone who is new to the subject, making them read selections from Kant's *Critique of Pure Reason,* Hegel's *The Phenomenology of Spirit,* or Heidegger's *Being and Time* is like learning to swim by being thrown into the ocean during a storm. In contrast to that, this book will attempt to take the most difficult areas of human inquiry and make them accessible to the average person.

Second, this book is relatively short. Some introductions to philosophy are over one thousand pages. (It is ironic that they are allowed to even be called introductions at that length). As you can imagine, one thousand pages can be a bit overwhelming for the average voter, businessman, college student, or busy mother who just wants to learn how to be a better thinker. I have made this book extremely short. *However, the cost for not having to read as much (quantity) is that you will have to read the book slowly (quality).* Please read that previous sentence again. The cost of keeping the book short is that it packs a punch, and you need to make sure you do not rush through it. My hope is that it will be like a good bourbon. There is a lot of flavor packed into a small glass. You should sip it, don't water it down, get past the burn, and then sit back and enjoy the incredible flavor profile.

Third, I have intentionally written this book in a normal, conversational tone. I've tried to avoid jargon as much as possible, and I've tried to keep it joyful, light, and engaging. A few sections even sound a little goofy. This is all intentional. Philosophy should be fun, and it should be fun to read. Though it is less "professional" to write in this style, it is easier to understand something written in a playful tone. In fact, Aristotle (whom we will meet later) even thought that wittiness and cleverness were moral virtues. It is righteous to be playful at times! So, I will seek to be virtuous in my writing style throughout the book.

Additionally, the writing style of this volume will feel a bit like it jumps from point to point or question to question. This is also intentional. When one is doing philosophy, one notices that when they are thinking of an idea another idea will often rush onto the scene to interrupt the previous idea. For example, one may be thinking about whether or not self-defense is ethical and then think of a time when someone tried to provoke them to a fight. One thought seems to randomly lead to another thought. However, it is not random. My hope is to show the reader the natural flow of doing philosophy. This includes walking a discernable path but not being afraid to take a few rabbit trails along the way.

Finally, the book tries to teach through asking a lot of questions and giving thought experiments instead of making a sustained case for certain positions. In my opinion, this is a better way to teach than if I were just to give you the "answers" to each question. Teaching people to just "parrot" one's answer is not a real education. People must learn *how* to think, not just *what* to think. Throughout the book, I will not give you my positions on most of the difficult questions we will encounter. It is not because I don't hold a position; I usually do. It is because you should, as Horace quipped, *sapere aude* (think for yourself)!

There is no book that doesn't have an agenda (a very philosophical thing to say), but I've tried to minimize my biases as much as possible. Can I fully get rid of my philosophical biases and preconceived agendas? No, I cannot. For example, I want to sell a million copies of the book so I can go live in Fiji. I want you to like my book because I'm insecure. I want to teach you to think critically so you don't go along with the unthinking masses. These are all biases that I have. We can't fully get rid of our presuppositions (even thinking that you can is, itself, a presupposition). We can, however, be aware of our agendas and seek to minimize them in our speaking and writing. By my attempts to keep the book "neutral," more people can engage with the thoughts contained therein without feeling like I'm browbeating them into holding some position. Someone who is an atheist would benefit from this book, but so would a religious believer. A liberal will appreciate some viewpoints, but a conservative will appreciate others. Whether you are a Democrat, Republican, Whig, Tory, Labor Party, Green Party, or even Teddy Roosevelt's "Bullmoose Party," there is a little something for everyone in this short volume.

What is the purpose of this book?

The purpose of this book is not to give extended backgrounds into every famous philosopher we will introduce. It is not to try to answer every philosophical question that we will examine. I did not write it so that you could quickly and easily find *my* answers to life's biggest questions. *Rather, its central purpose is to produce intellectual humility by showing us how little we really know.* It is to help us question our assumptions and teach us that things are much more difficult (and complex) than we initially assume.

The primary benefit of philosophy, as Bertrand Russell wrote in *The Problems of Philosophy*, is not so much its ability to find all the answers. Rather, it is the questions that it poses, the way it makes you think about the world, and the logical and critical thinking skills that it bestows upon you. Its benefit is that it quickly shoots down the person who is overconfident in what he thinks he knows. As legend would have it, this is why the Oracle at Delphi prophesied that Socrates was the wisest man alive. This statement was not because Socrates had all the answers. Rather, it was because

Socrates, unlike all the opponents he intellectually embarrassed, knew *how little* he actually knew.

Philosophy won't let you pretentiously take things for granted. Philosophy won't allow for lazy, imprecise, or sloppy thinking. Philosophy makes you work. *It is only after you have read, written, wrestled, doubted, become confused, been beaten in an argument, questioned God, fallen into despair, lost friends, challenged your deepest beliefs, and thrown something across the room in anger that you have begun to do philosophy.*

We haughtily assume that humanity today is smarter than humanity was in the past. We assume that because we have advanced in things such as medicine and technology that we have also advanced in things such as logical reasoning, morality, or justice. Nothing could be farther from the truth. Whereas children in ancient Athens used to debate the meaning of existence, our kids play Xbox. Whereas universities in the Middle Ages required monks to devote their entire life to formal study while debating professors, remaining single, living on campus for over a decade, knowing logic, mathematics, rhetoric, philosophy, theology, and doing everything in Latin, today you can get a business degree online so you can pat yourself on the back and get a piece of paper to add to your résumé.

Part of the reason our culture is so divided among political lines is due to intellectual arrogance. Nobody wants to sit down and do the difficult work of really challenging what they hold. We will do almost anything to avoid admitting that we were wrong or that we held a stupid position. Realizing that we might not be as smart as we think we are is the first step in coming to the table. It will allow us to better talk with our opponents, try to understand, and see who really has the better case for their position.

A little logic

Since I've already written an entire book on logic, I will keep this chapter short and not seek to repeat that information here.[3] Logic is a vast and powerful subject; it is the cornerstone of philosophy. Before we begin our journey into philosophy we don't need to know everything about philosophical logic. Rather, we simply need to focus on the primary rule of logic: *don't break the law of noncontradiction.*

Every time we make a statement, that statement is either true or false. Remember that a statement contains a subject and a predicate. Not all sentences are statements, but all statements are sentences. When we make a statement, also called a proposition, *that statement must be true or false— but not both at the same time and in the same way.* More technically, the law of noncontradiction is that something cannot both *be* and *not be* in the same way at the same time.

If I say "my name is Zach" or "two plus two is four" or "Atlanta has a baseball team," those statements are either true or false. But they cannot be both true and false at the same time. If you think a proposition can be both true and false at the same time, *then you have changed the meaning of at least one of the terms* somewhere along the way. I cannot say, "There is a chair, and there is not a chair, and both of those claims are true at the same time and in the same way." Well, obviously I can say the words (I just typed them, after all), but I wouldn't be saying anything *meaningful*, because I would be contradicting myself. Contradiction is the death knell of a philosopher. Contradiction is the destruction of all good things. *If you are caught in a contradiction it means that you hold two beliefs that fight against one another, so you are logically and necessarily wrong in something that you hold.*

Notice how we intuitively see that the law of noncontradiction is true. I cannot both affirm something and deny something while meaning the same thing by that "something." This law is not something I can prove by going back further in my reasoning. We see that the law of noncontradiction is *self-proving*. It is where we start. It doesn't have a further foundation; it is the foundation. It must be true. All truth is built on the idea of noncontradiction.

Perhaps you don't agree with this. Perhaps you think that something can be true and false at the same time and in the *exact* same way. But you would be wrong. If you were to say "It is true that we can break the law of noncontradiction," I would simply say, "Then it is also false that we can break the law of noncontradiction." And by simply saying that, I've beaten you at your own game. You cannot break the law of noncontradiction. If you could break the law of noncontradiction, then you could also not break the law of noncontradiction at the same time. *You even need the law of noncontradiction to try to disprove the law of noncontradiction.*

As we begin our journey into philosophy we will keep this in mind. Each time we discuss a particular position, we want to avoid contradicting ourselves. The law of noncontradiction will help protect us from going astray as we consider these difficult topics. Let's pause for a second to simplify what we have just discussed.

All we are trying to do is to find out what is true. The philosopher's job is to try to be right in whatever position she holds. If we want to be right, then we don't want to be wrong—even that itself follows the law of noncontradiction. Perhaps you think it is wrong or unloving to want to be right. Even that is a philosophical claim. If you say "it is unloving to care about being right," you would then be implying that the phrase "it is not unloving to care about being right" is false. You see? You can't get away from the law of noncontradiction.

Throughout our study our goal will be to come to conclusions that don't contradict other things we believe. We want to have a consistent viewpoint on whatever topic we are studying. By making sure that we don't think that true things are false and false things are true, we will be using logic to guide our way.

Dare to wrestle with philosophy

There are many in-depth, technical introductions to philosophy out there. If you want to go deeper, then I'd recommend one of those.[4] This book is just an appetizer. This book is just to get you going. This book will help give you a skeleton to which other textbooks can attach philosophical muscle.

This book will not help you master Athena, the ancient Greek goddess of wisdom. But it will help you take her out on a date. It will allow you to buy her dinner; it will help you flirt with her; it may even cause you to buy a ring in the hope that, one day, she will be yours. But nobody can master philosophy. Nobody can wed Minerva. She is too exhaustive in what she knows. She is too smart and too wise and too overwhelming in her knowledge. But this book will be an introduction to wisdom. You won't arrive, but it will teach you how to court Athena. And the first thing you need to know about Athena is that she is not led by emotion. She is a very logical lady.

Reality

This is your last chance. After this, there is no turning back. You take the blue pill—the story ends, you wake up in your bed and believe whatever you want to believe. You take the red pill—you stay in Wonderland and I show you how deep the rabbit hole goes.

—Morpheus, *The Matrix*

AFTER LOGIC, METAPHYSICS IS arguably the most all-encompassing area of philosophy. *Metaphysics is the study of reality.* It is the study of what exists. It is the study of what things really are. Metaphysics, as we use the term in philosophy, should not be confused with the way that term is used in many contemporary bookstores. If someone is being "metaphysical" they are usually being weirdly spiritual. Paranormal activity, New Age astrology, witchcraft, or some types of occult knowledge sometimes get labeled "metaphysics." The metaphysics section in any bookstore is not about Plato or Aristotle but about how to talk to the dead, how to conjure up a lost loved one, or some dumb vampire novel for teenagers.

That is not what the term means in philosophy. The term *metaphysics* comes from two Greek words: *meta* (after) and *physis* (nature). Metaphysics centers around the teachings of Aristotle that came *after* his teaching on nature/physics (hence, after-physics or *meta-physics*). Sometimes referred to as ontology (the study of *ontos*, or "being" in Greek) or first philosophy (because it addresses what is most real), metaphysics deals with the ultimate nature of everything.

Being

What is it that truly exists? If I were to ask you to name some things out in the world that you think exist, what types of things would you name? Perhaps you would say, "Trees exist." You would be right. Trees (except for the most dogmatic skeptic or anti-tree conspiracy theorist) do indeed exist. Perhaps you would say, "Mountains exist." You would also be right. Perhaps you would say, "The sun exists." Or perhaps you would say, "Animals exist." Or perhaps you would say, "Rocks exist." Or perhaps you would say, "The book that I am now reading exists."

Though I'm tempted to spend the next hundred pages listing objects that exist (as it would eventually become comical), I'm not going to do that. That would take quite a bit of time. You get the point. You could name a lot of things that you believe exist.

In each of the examples above, what we have agreed exist are *individual, material objects*. Though in philosophy there are always people on the fringes who would disagree with claims like "trees exist," most people would agree that these things, listed above, do actually exist. But here is where metaphysics starts to get tricky—what about things that are not material objects?

For example, does the *number* two exist? Let me clarify what I'm asking: I'm not asking if the *numeral* 2 exists. That numeral certainly exists. (If you don't believe me, just reread the above sentences and see where I wrote down the numeral, "2," thus making it exist). That is not my question. *A numeral is not the same as a number.* A numeral is an image—a mark that we make on a piece of paper—that supposedly refers to the actual number. We can see a numeral, but we cannot see a number. A numeral is a picture of a number, not the number itself. This is why we can signify the number two by writing: two, 2, II, one less than three, deux, or dos. The symbol or word can change, but they all refer to the same concept: the whole number that is in between one and three.

Back to our question: Does the actual number two exist? If you believe the number two exists, think of all that implies. Your view would imply that that there are an infinite number of things in the universe (that actually exist) that take up no space, are not made of any matter, and that cannot be perceived with the senses. Just by agreeing to the fact that the actual number two exists, you have opened up your metaphysical system to an entire world of things that are not made of matter. Should we really believe in things that we cannot see, taste, or touch? Should we really believe in things that no scientist can look at under a microscope? *If numbers exist, what else might exist that is not material?*

Perhaps you don't think that numbers exist. Perhaps your answer is "No, the number two does not exist; there can be only two material objects (sticks, dollars, etc.) but no actual number two." If that's your position, then what the heck are you even talking about by saying the word *two* with your mouth? How can you talk meaningfully about the number two if it doesn't exist? *If the number two doesn't exist, then why does math work so well and why do humans universally use counting*? Why do we have such a strong sense that numbers really do exist independently of our mental images of them?

Or here is another thought experiment. Do propositions exist? Not all sentences are propositions. "Why don't you study more philosophy?" or "Get back in your car" are sentences, but they are not propositions (one is a question and the other is a command). Propositions are sentences that put together a subject and a predicate. They name a state of affairs. Propositions are sentences like "A quarter is worth twenty-five cents," "Tacos are delicious," or "Nickelback is a terrible band." Propositions can be either true or false. What do propositions have to do with metaphysics (other than the fact that when we make claims in metaphysics we are always using propositions)? The interesting answer is that *propositions seem to be immaterial.* They seem to be something that exists that is not physical.

Consider the proposition "No bachelors are married." That is a true sentence; it is a true proposition. By definition, if someone is a bachelor, then they are not married. Take careful note of what the sentence is claiming. Bachelors exist, and they are physical. Married people exist, and they are material. The soundwaves that move when someone says the sentence "No bachelors are married," exist and they are material. But the proposition "No bachelors are married" (which has a logical truth value) exists and seems to be immaterial. The sentence as it is written on a piece of paper is written with material ink. *But the concept—the proposition itself—seems to be immaterial.*

Or consider something like an action. Does *running* exist? Does *swimming* exist? Does *existing* exist? Again, to clarify, I'm not asking if there are *people* who do the act of running or swimming. I'm not asking if there are people who exist. Those would be individual, material beings like we mentioned earlier. I'm asking, in addition to the individual Olympic athlete that is (at least partially) made of matter, is there something that exists that is not made of matter at all but rather made of *action*? An action may involve matter (to run one must have a body), *but the action itself is not the same as the matter.* Would we, from a modern point of view, say that running exists in the same way that trees exist? Is the universe composed of planets and stars and protons and *running*?

Or what about relations that seem to be immaterial. Relations are things like "beside," "under," or "near." Do these exist? If they do, do they exist in the same way that individual objects exist? In addition to the fact that there are trees, does the fact that the trees are *beside* each other mean that *beside-ness* (to use a made-up term) exists in the same way that an individual tree exists? Or what about bigness? When we made our list above we mentioned that the sun exists, but the sun happens to be really big. Does this mean that bigness is something that exists in the same way that the sun does? You can't just say no or yes to these difficult questions. You have to make a case for why you think relations do or do not exist.

To all the romantics out there reading this book, what about something like love? Does *love* exist? Again, I'm not asking if there are feelings that people subjectively have toward one another that they call love. I'm not asking if there are brain chemicals that make us feel butterflies in our stomach that we then call the English word *love*. I'm not asking if there are two physical *people* who love each other. *I'm asking if love itself exists.* Is there an objective entity, love, that really exists, or do we just call the internal emotions we have by the name *love*? *Would love still exist even if there were no humans or animals to feel love*? Furthermore, if love were just an emotion, is that emotion something other than chemical reactions in the brain? Is an emotion itself (not the chemical reaction in the brain) something that is real like a tree, or is it *nothing other than* chemical reactions in the brain that we perceive as strong affections for another?

What about dreams? If you think too much about dreams it can cause you to freak out. Dreams are really weird. Your body goes unconscious and you create an entire world in your mind that you think is "real" until you wake up.

Let's say one night, while you are asleep, you dream about living in your dream home (pun). In this dream you live in a beautiful mansion on top of a mountain range. You have bedrooms, bathrooms, and a living room in this house. On the walls you even have famous paintings from all over the world. Is this house that you have conjured up while you were sleeping "real"? If you say no, then I would ask, "How then did you spend several hours living in a dream house (walking from room to room and looking at the art on the wall) that didn't exist *in any sense*?" Surely it at least existed as a dream. I'm not asking if the house in your dream exists with as much "realness" as your actual house. I'm asking if it exists in any sense. All this leads to the conundrum of whether or not there can be different levels of reality. Does existence come in gradations? Or does your dream house exist at the same level as your real house?

Are you beginning to see why metaphysics may be a bit more complex than you initially assumed? Most people have never thought about reality like this. But we are not yet done; it gets even worse!

In metaphysics, we must consider tricky questions like: How the heck can you think of something that doesn't exist? Let's take, for example, Ares, the Greek god of war. Ares doesn't exist. (No offence to those who might be ardent Ares worshippers.) If it is true that Ares doesn't exist, then how did the ancient Greeks worship him? How did they think of him? Can you think of a non-existing thing? The sentence "Ares was married to Aphrodite" seems to have real meaning. But how could it have real meaning if neither the mighty Ares nor the gorgeous Aphrodite exist? Perhaps we just mean something like "According to Greek mythology, these two gods were married." But that just pushes the question back. To whom are we referring when we say "these two gods" if neither of them exists? Are we thinking of nothing? Are we just playing linguistic games?

The problems dealt with in metaphysics (being, reality, existence, etc.) give us labyrinths that both religious and nonreligious people have to solve. Consider, for example, free will. Does free will exist? Or what about God? Does he exist? What about the human soul? Does it exist? A religious person would probably affirm that all of these exist to some degree (though *none* of these things are material objects). An atheist would probably deny all three of them (usually *because* they are not material objects). But either answer runs into other metaphysical problems. How can humans have free will if everything is determined by material physics? And, if there is no soul, then what makes us "us," since all our physical cells change many times over our lifetime? If God exists, how might his existence be different than, say, a mountain or a physical house? If he doesn't exist, then how would you ever prove that claim, since you couldn't use scientific methods to perceive a being that is not material? If he does exist, then how does what is infinite and immaterial (God) interact with what is finite and material (the universe)?

You may have noticed that I haven't actually answered any of these intriguing questions. The point of these inquiries is to get you to question your assumptions. We tend to think of individual, concrete, material objects that we perceive with our senses as the only things that are real. That may indeed be right. But perhaps there are a whole host of things out there (in different categories) that also exist, even though they are not material. Or perhaps they are material and we have simply made a category mistake along the way by ascribing to them nonphysical properties.

What is most basic or real?

In a very real sense, metaphysics tries to discover the ultimate truth behind everything that exists: "What is there and of what are things made?" is the central question of metaphysics. What is the "stuff" that stands behind everything that exists? This may sound like an easy answer, but it is really difficult. You may say that everything is made up of atoms, but then what about things like numbers, concepts, actions, qualities, relations, subjective conscious experiences, and a host of other things that may exist that are not made of atoms? What about a vacuum of empty space? Does that vacuum "exist," and if so, what is it (since it cannot be made of atoms)? If a vacuum doesn't exist, then what do we mean by talking about empty space? Does space just mean nothingness? How can you talk about nothingness like it is something? *Nothing, by definition, is not something.*

Or perhaps I can rephrase the question this way: "Out of what is everything made?" Again, you may be tempted to say atoms, but that just pushes the question back further. Out of what are atoms made? You may say something like quarks or protons, neutrons, and electrons. But that still doesn't answer my question. Of what are quarks made? Of what are electrons made? And if you just say nothing, then you must realize that *you didn't actually answer my question; you simply decided to stop thinking when it became inconvenient for your theory.* You continued to give different English names to these tiny theoretical entities and then just decided to stop once you ran out of terms for these leptons. Are quarks material or immaterial? If you say quarks are made of "matter," then I'll ask, "And of what is that 'matter' made?" This leads us back to square one.

Isn't even a quark made up of two half-quarks and a half-quark made up of two quarter-quarks and a quarter-quark made up of two eighth-quarks? Can't you, at least *conceptually,* continue dividing quarks forever? If you can conceptually divide something forever, then you never get to the smallest thing in the universe (there would be no smallest thing in the universe). You can give as many names as you want to whatever it is that you think makes up everything else, but that doesn't actually answer my question. *I'm not asking what name scientists today call what they think is the smallest thing.* Those names change over time. What they now call quarks used to be called atoms, and before that they were called corpuscles. I'm asking, "Out of what are these supposed scientific entities (themselves) made, and is it just one thing?"

Throughout the history of philosophy there have been many attempts to try to take everything that exists and "boil it down" to what is most basic. There have been many answers given to the question of what makes up everything else. Some of the earliest metaphysicians chose one of the four elements as candidates for the basic building blocks of the universe. When we hear that there were people who used to think that the most basic elements where things like fire or air, we have a tendency to scoff at how elementary (pun) that is. But these brilliant thinkers were trying to answer this enormous question without microscopes, electricity, and the internet. As we will see, their answers are smarter than you may imagine.

For example, Thales said everything was made of water. After all, ice is made of water, coffee is made of water, lettuce is about 96% water, animals are mostly water, trees are mostly water, clouds are made of water, and most of the world is covered with water. When water gets hot it becomes a gas (thus explaining air), and when it gets cold it becomes a solid (thus explaining earth). Human semen is a liquid, so even humans, in a sense, are produced from water (not to mention our bodies are primarily water). When you stop and think about it, water was not a terrible option for Thales to have picked!

We have a tendency to think that these ancient assumptions are naive and unsophisticated. But it is important to note two things: First, what thinkers like Thales were doing was trying to find one, universal "stuff" out of which everything is made. *They were just like scientists today who think that everything is made of matter.* They were doing metaphysics at the highest level. Second, their answers (though probably wrong) were very well reasoned.

Though the pre-Socratic (the philosophers who came before Socrates) proposals sound strange to us, our views would have sounded equally strange to them. Allow me to explain with a quick hypothetical dialogue between our friend, Thales, and a twenty-first-century college student.

> Thales: Everything is water.
>
> Student: That's dumb, surely this book I'm reading isn't made of water.
>
> Thales: Why don't you think it is made of water?
>
> Student: Because it looks nothing like water!
>
> Thales: Of what do you think it is made?
>
> Student: Atoms.
>
> Thales: What are atoms?
>
> Student: Atoms are tiny spheres swirling around in empty space.
>
> Thales: But the book looks nothing like tiny spheres and space either . . .

Student: What do you mean?

Thales: You critiqued my view that the book was made of water because it looks nothing like water, but then said it was made of atoms, though the book looks nothing like atoms either.

The point of this quick back-and-forth is to try to understand *why* ancient thinkers came to the conclusions they did and to show that many of the supposed "answers" we give today still need to be pushed further.

Though Thales thought everything was water, other thinkers gave other answers. Anaximenes said everything was made of air. Heraclitus said everything was ultimately made of fire. Democritus said that everything was made of tiny atoms. (See? We are not as clever today as we think.) Anaximader said that everything is made of an indefinite stuff called *aperion*. Pythagoras, that guy whose boring theorem you had to memorize in school, thought that numbers were the most real things in the universe (because they are eternal).

In all these attempts, brilliant people were trying to find out what is most real. This isn't the case with only philosophers known as the pre-Socratics. Plato thought the most real things were a higher level of ideas called forms. Aristotle thought that everything was made up of individual substances. Anselm thought that the most real thing was a necessarily existent God. Berkeley thought that everything was made up of minds that perceive. Leibniz thought everything was made up of preprogrammed, separate, mental substances called monads. Spinoza thought that everything was part of a panentheistic but absolute, all-encompassing *deus sive natura* (God or nature). Hegel thought that everything was part of a universal evolving spirit (German: *Geist*). Alfred North Whitehead thought that everything was event. As you can see, it is very difficult to choose just one thing that is the most "real" thing in the universe.

So I now pose the question to you: *What do you think makes up everything else*? Or perhaps it is more than one thing. Surely a tree is not made of the same "stuff" as the number two, an idea, or God. Or is it? Or do those things not *really* exist?

Metaphysics before Socrates was fascinating and clever. Most historians of philosophy, however, begin what we think of today as Western philosophy with Socrates and his more prolific disciple, Plato.

Plato and Forms

Socrates was the teacher of Plato. Plato was the teacher of Aristotle. Aristotle was the teacher of Alexander the Great. That is quite a pedigree for our superstud, Alexander. No wonder he conquered the ancient world in his twenties. He is not called Alexander the Pretty Good. He stood in a tradition that was, up until that time, the greatest system of philosophy every invented.

Though much fascinating philosophy happened before Socrates, it is really with Socrates that we see the rigorous back-and-forth dialectic that we consider "philosophy" and rational argumentation. Since we don't have Socrates direct writings, and because Socrates becomes the mouthpiece for Plato's dialogues, it is Plato who will become our starting point in Western philosophy. It should be noted that Plato is probably the most influential philosopher of all time. In fact, the famous Harvard logician Alfred North Whitehead commented that basically all of Western philosophy was simply "footnotes to Plato."[5]

Plato's student, however, would go on to rival his fame. His name is Aristotle, and his thought would become the starting point for modern science. The thought of these two great thinkers is too vast to fully explore in a short introduction to philosophy. We will therefore explore their central metaphysical disagreement with a few thought experiments. Let's move chronologically by beginning with Plato before transitioning to Aristotle.

Though Plato preferred to talk about major ideas like beauty, justice, and goodness, I'm going to start by using an example he probably wouldn't like (because I think it is easier to explain to new philosophy students). I'm going to use the example of a table. Again, Plato wouldn't focus on a man-made artifact like a table, but we will start with this simple illustration before moving onto things that he would consider actual "forms."

Consider a table. We all know what a table is. You may even be reading this book at a table right now. *What is it that makes a table a table*? That may sound like a silly question, so let's take that question (and table) apart, piece by piece. If you have a table that has four legs and a top, is that a table? You will probably say, "Of course that is a table." Okay, so far, so good; a four-legged table with a top is indeed a table. If I take away one of the legs of the table, is it still a table? Yes, you can indeed have a three-legged table. So far, so good. Now let's say I take away another leg so there are only two legs . . . is it still a table? You will probably still say yes. After all, you could prop a table with two legs up against a wall and you would still have a table. But what if I took away the top part of the table and all you were left with was two table legs and no top? Do you still have a table? At this point you would probably say no. You were comfortable saying that a table with fewer legs was still a table, but when the top of the table is removed, you would say that there is no more table.

Here is the million-dollar question: *How did you know that? How did you know the standard definition of "table-ness" before we even finished the thought experiment?* How did you know that some changes allowed the table to remain a table? How did you know that other changes didn't allow the table to remain a table? What is it that makes a table truly a table?

You may be inclined to say that the tabletop is what made it a table, but that is not true. After all, a tabletop is literally just a flat piece of wood. Every flat piece of wood is not a table (such as a piece of particleboard you see on the ground at a construction site). So that can't be the answer. Or maybe you thought that what made the table a table was its *function*: it holds food for you while you eat. But that doesn't work either. After all, many tables exist that aren't for food (such as a conference table used in a military briefing room). Furthermore, you can eat food on a plate that is sitting on your lap or on the floor, but neither your lap nor the floor (nor the plate!) is a table.

Let's consider something more abstract than a table. Consider a square. We all know what a square is. But, like most things in philosophy, when we think hard about something, what we think we know begins to get fuzzy. We don't encounter any perfect squares in the real world. By saying "we don't encounter any perfect squares in the real world," I don't mean that we just have trouble drawing squares because our hands always shake a little bit when drawing. Rather, I mean that a square is just a concept that *cannot actually exist in the physical world even if a machine were drawing straight lines without shaking.* What do I mean? Allow me to explain.

A square is a shape with four equal sides (lines) and four right angles. But here is where it becomes mind-blowing: *all squares in the physical world have lines that have thickness, but a true line doesn't have thickness.* If you zoom in far enough on any line, you will see that it has breadth to it. It has thickness. *But a true line cannot have thickness or it is not a line.* A line is, by mathematical definition, made up of points. But how big is a point? *The answer is that a point doesn't have a size.* If you think that a point has a size, then it is no longer a point but a tiny, tiny plane. (If you zoom in on a period at the end of a sentence in this book, you'll notice that it isn't an actual point but rather a small, flat plane that gets bigger the more you zoom in.) A point (like a line) is just a *concept*; it is not spatial. *Here we see that an actual, perfect square doesn't exist down here in the concrete world of sense perception.* The true perfect *form* of the square (the perfect definition that we have given above) is different than square-like objects we encounter in the world such as Post-it notes, chess boards, and Scrabble pieces.

The rabbit hole goes even deeper. How do you know what a square is if you have never actually encountered a real, true, perfect, lines-with-no-thickness square in your day-to-day life? If someone were to draw a square and make it slightly too tall, you would immediately know that it is no longer a square but a rectangle. How did you know that? You might be tempted to say that your teacher taught you about the difference between squares and rectangles when you were a kid. But that just pushes the question back further. How did your teacher know that it was a rectangle? Well, their teacher told them. But what about the very first person to ever know what a square was? How did they know they were right? You might say they just made it up. Some caveman just decided to call a square a "square" in whatever caveman language they had back then. But we are not asking where the word for square came from—that was invented by humans. We are asking where actual squareness comes from. The angles of a square always equal 360 degrees. This is an unchanging fact about squares even if no humans had ever decided to draw squares on their own and even if we had never decided to call them squares. It is a fact that seems to be something that has always been true even before any humans viewed squares. To say it one more time, how do we know what makes a rectangle different than a square if we have no perfect rectangles or squares to be our standard definition of these shapes?

For Plato, the reason that you knew what a table was (again, not an example Plato would have liked) and what a square was (an example that Plato would have loved) is because reality is bifurcated into two realms. There is the realm of the forms and the realm of individual objects "down here" that we experience. *Think of a form as the standard definition for what something really is.* Oftentimes you will see the term *form* written with a capital *F* just to make the point (i.e., *Form*). The reason you know what a square is has to do with the fact that there is a form of squareness up in a higher realm above us (that is more real than what we experience down here). The square napkins at a bar that we experience down here are merely shadows, imperfect and changing representations of the eternal form of a Square that has always existed.

It was essential for Plato that we know that there has to be a standard definition of things so we can truly know any particulars down here on earth. For example, consider a little kid who has never seen a horse. Upon seeing a horse, the child says, "Daddy, what is that animal?" That dad replies, "That is a horse." That sounds simple enough, but here is the problem that Plato would point out: *How does the child know the dad is right?* How did the dad know it was a horse? Again, we are not asking about the English name *horse*. We are asking about actual "horse-ness" or what truly makes an animal a horse instead of a hippo or a crocodile. How would the child test the dad's claim that the animal they are viewing is indeed a horse unless the child already knew what a horse was? Second, how could a child learn what a horse was unless he already had some knowledge of the horse in him? How could that first image "stick" if there were not already a pattern to which it could "stick"? Again, I'm using things like tables and horses to teach a lesson. Plato preferred to think of forms as much bigger categories like Truth (capital *T*) and Goodness (capital *G*). (There is some debate by scholars of Plato on what types of things truly had forms.)

How do we know these forms? How are they already inside us? Plato believed that human souls were eternal and that we had known the forms back in eternity. For Plato, we had once known the forms but had since forgotten them. All learning, for Plato, is more like remembering something we once knew instead of learning it for the first time. In Plato's work *The Meno*, an uneducated slave is called over to a man who shows him how to reason to all kinds of mathematical truths. Though the boy is uneducated, after just a few sentences the boy is able to solve all kinds of mathematical equations. By using this example Plato is trying to show that our knowledge of unchanging truths (like mathematics) is already in us. We may think we learn that two plus two equals four, but once we know that, we can also figure out that two plus three equals five, though nobody actually taught us this new equation! We were somehow able to figure it out. Once we knew a few numbers, we were able to extrapolate many more. How were we able to do this?

If you are confused, let's look at Plato's view of the forms from another angle. Clear your mind for a second, take a big breath, and let's start over.

Perhaps we could ask a question like this: *Is beauty objective*? Is "beauty in the eye of the beholder," or is it truly objective? Is there a standard or *form* of beauty? When a man finds a woman beautiful, is that because she takes part in the objective, unchanging standard of beauty itself or just because he subjectively thinks she looks nice? Conversely, when a woman thinks that a man looks handsome, is this because he takes part in the objective, unchanging standard of beauty or just because she subjectively thinks he looks nice?

Or, to move away from people, consider a mountain in Colorado. Imagine a snowcapped mountain with a crystal clear lake at the bottom. There are pine trees all around, and mist is rising up over the water on an incredible spring morning. Is this scenery objectively beautiful, or is beauty just "in the eye of the beholder"? This is a difficult question. On the one hand we want to say that beauty is subjective. One person finds the image of the mountain beautiful, while, perhaps, another person does not. *Is that because beauty is subjective or because the person who thinks mountains are ugly is objectively wrong in their opinion of what is beautiful?* "But wait," you may say, "someone can't be wrong in their opinion on what they think is beautiful." According to Plato, someone can absolutely be wrong in their opinion if that opinion is contrary to fact. Not just facts but opinions can be wrong; if a person's opinion was that two plus two equals five, that would be an objectively wrong opinion. Plato would say the same for beauty.

Let's consider another example. Imagine a beautiful sunset. If someone thought that a majestic, brilliant, purple-and-gold sunset was ugly, is that merely "true for them" (a subjective claim), or is the sunset actually beautiful (an objective claim)? Could it be the case that this sunset-hating person's ability to know what is and is not beautiful is somehow broken or distorted?

Most of us want to say that beauty is subjective. One person likes a sunset and another person doesn't like it. One person thinks a piece of artwork is gorgeous and another doesn't really see it. But there are a lot of problems with denying that beauty is actually objective. If you say that beauty is not objective, you have to say that there is no standard of beauty whatsoever. *You have to say that the child murderer who thinks pictures of dead children are beautiful is not wrong.* You have to say that the shock artist who puts his grandmother's skull in a tub of urine and calls it "art" has made something beautiful if he merely proclaims that it's beautiful. You have to say that the Nazi guard at Auschwitz who finds it to be aesthetically pleasing to watch Jews be gassed alive is not wrong. What about evil people who find horrendous acts to be "beautiful" *to them*? Is it because they are actually beautiful, or is it because their minds are misperceiving the form of what true beauty is?

Conversely, if you say that beauty is objective, then it means some people are wrong in what they find to be beautiful. We don't like hearing that aesthetics may be objective. Do we want to believe that our baby may actually be objectively ugly? None of this is to say that Plato is correct. It is merely a thought experiment to contrast the objectivity of the forms with the actual individual objects that we can perceive with our senses. Plato is the king at making things conform to a higher standard.

Regardless of where you stand, the answer is easy for Plato. Aesthetics is objective, and something is beautiful or not based on whether or not it instantiates the form of beauty—whether or not it conforms to the universal, unchanging, eternal standard of beauty. For Plato, beauty exists up in the realm of the forms, and something is beautiful "down here" (sunsets, etc.) if it *participates* in that unchanging form of beauty. Sunsets are beautiful, and if someone thinks a sunset is ugly, it is because something is broken in their ability to discern the form of true beauty. The murderer who likes pictures of dead children is wrong, for Plato, because that is objectively not beautiful and doesn't conform to the standard of true beauty, which is above us.

I've used the example of beauty because it shocks our senses. But for Plato, things are true down here because they conform to the form of Truth. Things are good down here because they conform to the form of Goodness or the Good. We know that a yield sign is a triangle (down here) because it conforms to the form of Triangle.

What do you think of our friend Plato so far? Is Plato right? Many have thought that Plato's system is the greatest system of philosophy in history. For us to have knowledge, there must be a metaphysical level of things that are more real and unchanging (i.e., the forms). Others have adapted Plato a bit because they wanted to keep objective definitions for things but rid themselves of some of his metaphysical baggage. This is especially the case regarding Plato's influence on Christianity.

For example, the philosopher and theologian St. Augustine of Hippo adapted Platonic ideas (though he got them from Plotinus) so that they would better mesh with his religious faith. For Augustine, there are still objective definitions of things (i.e., forms), but they are definitions in the mind of God and not things that eternally exist up in a detached realm of forms. God knows what a triangle is, and the created triangles on earth participate in that definition. Additionally, since in Christian theology the soul is not eternal but has been made by God, Augustine thought we still have innate ideas (and that "learning" is really "remembering"), but *God puts these ideas in our minds when he creates us*; we do not eternally have them. Others, like Aristotle, completely disagreed with Plato.

Whereas Plato's view is very "otherworldly" with all his talk of forms and such, Aristotle's view is very "this-worldly." If one thinks of the famous painting known as the *School of Athens* by Rafael (not the ninja turtle with the red mask, but the painter), one sees Plato pointing up toward the eternal forms. Aristotle, walking beside him, has his hand extended toward the ground. One can imagine that they are having a debate about philosophy with Plato positing a top-down approach and Aristotle positing a bottom-up approach. Aristotle believed that forms were not in the "heavens." Rather, the form was in the individual thing itself. The triangle has triangle-ness in an individual triangle. The form, for Aristotle, is just what something is that makes it that thing. *Aristotle turns Plato's system on its head in that he thinks we start our intellectual journey by looking at the individual things down here on earth instead of looking toward the heavenly forms that are on another metaphysical plane.* Aristotle didn't think that one could bridge the gap in Plato's system. If the forms are perfect and eternal, how in the world can objects down here interact ("participate") with them? Because of that, he preferred to talk about what he called substances.

Aristotle and substance

For Aristotle, a substance is an individually existing thing. It is the thing that "stands under" things that change (which is what the word *sub-stance* means). The things that change are called many things in philosophy, but we can simply call them properties or even accidents. The word *accident* here does not mean that something went wrong (like when people have an automobile accident). It is called an accident because it is something that is *not necessary* (i.e., "accidental") to a substance. Some properties are necessary for a thing to be what it is. If a human were not really a human (but rather an alien in a human skin suit), that would certainly change the supposed substance of *human*. But other properties are not necessary for a thing to be what it is. A human can have hair or be bald, be tall or short, like the Dallas Cowboys or not like the Dallas Cowboys, and they are still a human. If that sounds confusing, then let's begin with an example.

An individual lion would be a substance. The lion is what "stands under" its properties. However, the fact that it has a mane is a property that can change. A lion could lose its mane and still be a lion. The fact that a lion is a brownish-gold color is a property that can change; it could be a different color, and the lion would still be a lion. (There are, after all, albino lions.) The lion could be bigger or heavier or angrier than it is and still be a lion. The lion is the substance; it is what "stands under" all the other properties and their changes. Or we could look at it this way. I am an individual man named Zach. If I lost my hair, I would still be the man, Zach. If I lost an arm, I would still be the man, Zach. If I were taller or shorter, I would still be the man, Zach. But if something more drastic were to be the case (if I were to become an angel or had been zapped and vaporized by a sci-fi weapon) then I would no longer be the man, Zach.

In Aristotle's own words from his work *Categories*:

> *Substance—strictly so called, primarily and par excellence—is that which is neither said of a subject nor is in a subject, e.g. such-and-such a man, such-and-such a horse. Second substances are the species and genera to which the primary substances belong. Thus, such-and-such a man belongs in the species human, and the genus of his species is animal; so both human and animal are called second substances.*[6]

To summarize Aristotle's tricky language with all his "such-and-such" jargon: I am both an animal and a human, but my truest substance (what Aristotle calls primary) is that I am the individual man, Zach.

But here is where a good skeptic will step in. A good skeptic will say, "But, Zach, you don't ever experience a 'substance'; you don't ever experience the thing 'under' or 'behind' the properties of things; *you experience only the properties.*" The skeptic will say that when we see a horse, we don't ever actually see the form of *horse-ness*; we never experience the substance. We experience *only* the properties. We see the horse's color. We see the horse's height. We see that the horse is a solid. But we never actually see the thing that stands behind all these properties. We don't see *horse-ness* but just brown, solidity, fur, etc. *How do we know that there is a substance at all?* Is a horse just a bundle of its properties? Is there no actual horse but just a collection of properties (any of which can change)? If a horse is just a bundle of properties, then perhaps we as humans are just bundles of properties and there is nothing enduring that makes us . . . well . . . us.

What do you think? Is a form above an individual object, on another metaphysical plane, or is it in the individual object? Are forms more top down or bottom up? Do we know that a horse is a horse because it participates in a standard of horse-ness (detached from any individual horse) or because we see several horses and generalize out from there?

The debate between Plato and Aristotle rages even to this day. Most philosophical systems go back to one of these two starting points. Deep down, every person leans toward either Plato or Aristotle even if they have never read either figure. It is incredible that the two most influential philosophers of all time were friends, that one was even taught by the other, and that they yet came to two very different conclusions.

How are you holding up so far? Are you glad you began a study in philosophy, or would it have been better to continue thinking that life is simple and that ignorance is bliss? There is a reason I began this chapter with a quote from *The Matrix*.[7] Philosophy has a tendency to wake people up from a banal existence and to expose them to a vivid world they had no idea existed. We have a few more topics to address in this chapter before moving into the fascinating topic of knowledge in the next chapter.

How many substances are there?

The philosophy done in the Middle Ages has often been pejoratively characterized as medieval monks debating how many angels can dance on the head of a pin. Not only did this debate never take place, it is actually a very important question! How on earth could beings who are supposed to be immaterial (angels) interact with things that are material (pinheads)? When someone thinks they saw an angel, how could they have seen something that doesn't have a physical body? The reason this is a difficult question is because it deals with how two very different substances (material pins and immaterial angels) can interact. If we think back to our good friend Casper the Friendly Ghost, we remember that (in the TV show and in the movie) he can apparently walk through walls. Why is that? Well, supposedly, his immaterial ghost substance isn't hindered by the material wall.

My purpose here is not to talk about ethereal substances, like ghosts. The truly haunting question is: *How can something that is immaterial interact with what is material?* For example, do we have "free will," or is everything materially determined? One item seems to be immaterial (our will), and the other seems to be material (our body and the causal forces acting upon it). Is there a God, and if so, how can an eternal, immaterial God interact with finite, material creation if the gap between the two is *infinite*? We intrinsically feel as though two substances that are completely different would have trouble interacting. How can mind interact with matter? How can something immaterial (or spiritual) interact with something that is physically solid?

If everything were immaterial, then this question would not arise; if everything were material, then this question would not arise. It might very well be the case that everything either is immaterial or everything is material. But what has intrigued philosophers for most of intellectual history is what is called *metaphysical dualism*. This is the idea that everything boils down to two basic underlying things: things that are material (and physical) and things that are immaterial (and not physical). But we are getting ahead of ourselves.

Let's back up and ask this question: How many different substances really exist? The short answer is that there are really only two options. Some think that there is only one substance that exits in the entire universe. These philosophers are called *monists*. Though some objects may look very different from other objects, at their core, they are made up of the same kind of "stuff." Others think that there is more than one substance that exists in the entire universe. These philosophers are called *pluralists*. Our buddy we mentioned earlier, Thales, is an example of a monist because he thought that everything was made of water. Heraclitus is also a monist. To Heraclitus, everything was fire. But there is a more famous monist named Baruch (Benedict) Spinoza.

Spinoza believed that two different substances could not interact. After all, we have already discussed that Casper can walk through walls and angels can dance on pinheads. If there were more than one substance, then there would be no way for your subjective experience to move your physical body. There would also be no way for God to interact with the world. Spinoza's grand conclusion is that everyone and everything is one, large substance, which he famously called "God or nature." *By this he means that he doesn't care what you call everything that exists as long as you know that there is only one true substance for everything that does exist.* By using the word *God*, Spinoza does not mean a personal God such as you find in traditional, releveled religion. Rather, God is simply the source of Being. For Spinoza, though God is more than nature, nature is in God.[8] His view is a panentheistic account of everything in the universe. Since there is only one substance, we don't run into the problem of how differing substances (plural) would interact. There is only one substance, which has both immaterial and material components.

Most scientists today are monists. They believe that there is one and only one thing that everything in the universe is made of—physicality. Strict materialism is technically in the same vein as Thales and Spinoza because it states that there is only one substance, only one type of "stuff" in the universe.

On the other hand, there are pluralists. These would include guys like René Descartes and Gottfried Leibniz. For Descartes, there are three main substances: God (infinite mind), mind, and body (notice that these philosophers are using the term *substance* in a broader way than Aristotle did). However, this runs into the problem of how these things can interact. How can our immaterial minds/souls move our physical bodies? Descartes didn't solve the problem of how they can interact (we will explore this more when we discuss mind and body in the chapter on self). For someone like Descartes (not to mention many other philosophers) there is more than one type of thing that exists. God is very different from the human mind, which is very different from something that is material, like one's fingernail or an asteroid.

Leibniz was also a pluralist and is on the complete opposite end of the spectrum from Spinoza. He was a pluralist in the strongest sense of the term. Leibniz believed that *everything that exists is a different substance from every other thing that exist,* and he called these varying substances *monads.* The monads don't actually interact with each other (because two different substances, by definition, cannot interact). Rather, they just *appear* to interact because God has preprogrammed all of them to do exactly what they do through what Leibniz called "preestablished harmony."

To give a crude example of what Leibniz was saying, pretend that I was a movie director and I wanted to film a scene involving robots that fought one another. I wouldn't have the robots actually try to fight and respond to one another. (I'm not sure how good robots are at learning jujitsu). Rather, I would have computer programmers program the robots to *look like* they were fighting. The programmers would tell robot A that it should lift its arm when robot B throws a punch. I would have robot A duck its head when robot B tries to karate-chop it. The programmers would choreograph a fight between two robots, but the two robots would not actually be reacting to each other—meaning, one robot would not be perceiving that the other robot was trying to punch him and then remember his robot jujitsu training. Rather, they are simply following motions that have been *preprogrammed* into them by computer programmers. They look like they are interacting, but they are not. The two different robots correspond in harmony due to what is in them (programming), not due to what is outside of them (causal reaction to one another). They don't really "see" each other, which is what Leibniz means by famously saying monads are "windowless."

How do the monads have their entire history programmed into them? Well, there is a supreme monad at the top, which is how Leibniz portrays God. This supreme substance is the one who programs all the other substances to relate to one another in a choreographed orchestra of what *appears* to be (but is not really) causal interaction.

Notice how dramatically different these two positions are. Someone like Thales, or Spinoza, or a pure materialist would say that everything is made up of one substance (water, or God, or matter, in these three cases). Someone like Leibniz would say that not only are things not made up of one substance, but everything that exists is its own, individual substance, and it does not literally, causally interact with other substances. Between these two extremes are about a million other options.

Where do you stand on this issue? Is everything made of one type of thing or several types of things? If you are a monist and you say one, then why are things so different? Are a tree and the number two made of the same stuff? If you are a pluralist and say more than one, how can things that are completely different from each other interact?

Idealism vs. materialism

Within the topic of metaphysics, we need to briefly mention the issue of idealism vs. materialism. Are the most basic elements that exist immaterial (like minds or consciousness), or are they material (like rocks or bodies)? Is one type of thing more real than another? Is everything mental, idea, and nonmaterial? Some people have advocated for this position because everything we experience (even supposed "matter") *we experience only in our minds.* Perhaps all that exists are minds and immaterial objects. Or, is everything material, corporeal, and physical? Some people have advocated for this position because it appears as though the only items we can perceive with our senses are physical. Or, is there some combination of the two? Perhaps some things are ideal and other things are material, but then we run into our continued problem of how they could possibly interact.

Neither position is without difficulties. The idealist is in the tricky spot of trying to convince us that much of what we assume about the world is not correct. As I type this sentence on my computer, I assume that my computer is made of matter, but I could be totally incorrect, as it could be a collection of monads or something that exists just as immaterial ideas in the mind of God. That view sounds a bit detached from common sense, but in philosophy we never get to dismiss an idea because it sounds crazy (but only if we can logically refute it).

The problem with the materialist, though, is also disturbing. If the only thing that exists is matter, then how do we know that the actual, material table is the same as the one that appears to us in our thought and experience of the table? After all, one table—the "actual" table—is supposedly outside of us, but the only place we can interact with it is in our mind. Additionally, if thoroughgoing materialism is true, then there is no such thing as free will. If the world is purely material, then everything is determined. The universe, functioning like a huge machine, can do only exactly what it did. Inputs are put into the cosmic machine, and we get only necessary outputs. There are no contingencies. If I am only a collection of atoms and I murder someone, I literally could not have refrained from murdering them. One atom moved another atom, which moved another atom, which changed chemicals in my brain, which then commanded my body to stab my victim to death. *The reason we sentence someone for murder is because we believe they could have done otherwise.* But that is not the case if materialism is true.

What do you think? Is the universe made up of only matter, only ideas/ experience, or a combination of both? Why?

Realism vs. nominalism

Let's briefly look at a debate that was especially important during the Middle Ages. Consider the color red. Would "redness" exist even if there were no individual red things down here on earth? Would the color red exist, even if there were no tomatoes, stop signs, or cardinals? *Is redness an actually existing entity, or is it just a name that we use to classify individual things that we put into the same category of things we call red?*

If you say redness is an actually existing entity, then you are a realist. A realist believes that there are real entities that exist even apart from us having any individual instantiations of them down here on earth. In fact, many realists would claim that the only reason you have any experience of red objects down here is just because the larger entity of redness exists (and the red objects down here simply conform to that universal standard). Someone like Plato was certainly a realist, becasue the mysterious forms existed before there were any material objects. However, many religious philosophers (Christian, Muslim, and Jewish) were also realists, because the standard definition of things must exist in the mind of God before he created any individual objects. God must have known redness before he made cardinals, for example.

On the other side of the spectrum you have nominalism. (If someone is a "nominal" Yankees fan, then that means they are a fan *in name only*.) A nominalist believes that we experience individual red things (a strawberry, blood, or roses) and we extrapolate out to the idea of redness. But redness would not exist apart from individual red things. By calling something red, we are saying that its category is a category *in name only* (hence the term *nominalism*), but the actual, independent category of redness does not exist on its own. Again, we see that a realist is more top down, and a nominalist is more bottom up. Many philosophers, both religious and irreligious, have been nominalists. Perhaps what exists in the mind of God is not a category of redness (apart from any red items) but merely the red items themselves that God knew he was going to create.

You see that metaphysics could be several volumes instead of a short chapter in a short book. But metaphysics deals with some of the biggest questions on which humans can think. Speaking of humans, let's end this chapter with another tricky issue that we must know in our thinking about metaphysics: the topic of identity.

Identity

When someone gives an analogy, the analogy breaks down at some point. If I say that a football player is "as strong as an ox," I don't mean to say that he is like an ox in every way. I don't mean that he has horns, weighs over a ton, or has hooves. I don't mean to say that he should pull a wagon or eat only hay (or whatever oxen eat). I mean to draw the analogy in only one place—the category of strength.

There is no such thing as a perfect analogy because, to be a *perfect* analogy, it would have to be the very object to which we are comparing it. The only thing that is *exactly* like my wife is my wife. Other women have green eyes and brunette hair, but they have only some features of my wife.

They may look a little like my wife, but only my wife, and she alone, is *exactly* like my wife.

I once had a philosophy professor who told a story about riding in the car with his children when they were young. One of his kids looked out the window on the highway and said, "Dad, look, there is a car exactly like ours." The professor said to his son, "You're right, buddy, that car is exactly like ours . . . except that it is over there and ours is over here . . . and they own that one and we own this one . . . and that one has slightly different wheels . . . and we are riding in this one and not in that one . . . and they were probably not made at the exact same time . . . apparently that car is not exactly like ours, is it?" Now, whether or not this is good parenting is another question (I'd argue that teaching your kids to think is excellent parenting). This example leads to the issue of identity. Can one car be "exactly" like another one if there is any difference at all?

Imagine that there are two cars. They are the exact same year, make, and model. They have all the same features. They are the same color. To the average person, there is nothing about them that seems different. Here is the tricky issue. If they are *exactly* the same, then how are they not just the same one car? If one object has *exactly* the same properties as another object, then it would be just one object. There is no such thing as two things being *exactly* alike, or else they would not really be two, distinct things. *For something to be identical to itself, it has to have all the same properties as itself.* In this example of the two cars, they actually are not the same car (despite being the same year, make, and model) because they don't have the *exact* same properties. For example, one of them is in a different location than the other one. One of them was probably made slightly before the other one. One of them is to the left of the other, and the other is to the right of that one.

For something to be identical with itself, it needs to have the same properties as itself. But what happens when one of these properties changes? Do you still have the same thing? For example, if you have a pen sitting on a desk near the edge, it has the property of "being near the edge." If I push the pen near the center of the table (and away from the edge), is it still the same pen? After all, I've changed a property by moving its location (and technically, the pen is now older than the previous pen when we started, because it took at least a fraction of a second to move it)? The answer to this question will depend on what you think about substances above. Does the pen remain the same because it is the same underlying substance and only changed an unimportant (accidental) property, or is it an entirely new pen? This question seems unimportant when talking about pens, but as we will see in a later chapter, it becomes really important when talking about what makes you "you" as your body changes overtime.

Conclusion

You'll notice that I've given very few answers in this chapter. But I hope I've given you enough questions to cause you to question what you thought you knew. We've covered questions like what is it that exists, how many substances exist, what even is a substance, are some things immaterial, what is identity, and many more.

Metaphysics is the philosophical category in which all the big boys and girls play. The greatest philosophers of all time each had elaborate systems of metaphysics. Since metaphysics is the study of reality, it is probably the biggest area of philosophy you want to get right. But, even if we held the correct view about what actually exists, how would we know we were right? After all, everything we experience (whether we think it is material or immaterial), we experience in our mind. How do I know that the horse that I perceive in my mind is the same as the actual horse that is out there in reality? To answer this, we have to look at metaphysic's twin sister, epistemology, which is the subject of our next chapter.

Knowledge

The demon, Screwtape: "By the very act of arguing, you awaken the patient's reason; and once it is awake, who can foresee the result? Even if a particular train of thought can be twisted so as to end in our favour, you will find that you have been strengthening in your patient the fatal habit of attending to universal issues and withdrawing his attention from the stream of immediate sense experiences. Your business is to fix his attending on the stream. Teach him to call it 'real life' and don't let him ask what he means by 'real.'"

—C. S. Lewis, *The Screwtape Letters*

EPISTEMOLOGY IS THE STUDY of knowledge. It comes from the Greek word *epistēmē*, which simply means "knowledge." Epistemology can be summarized with the question: "What do you know and how do you know what you know?" We all think we know a great many things, but as we will find out, proving that you have good reasons for why you think you know something is trickier than expected.

Let's hit the ground running by returning to another thought experiment we introduced in the last chapter: How do you know that you are not in a dream right now?

You think you're not in a dream, but there are many times before that you thought you were not in a dream (when you actually were). In dreams that you have previously had, there were other people, conversations, locations, and hosts of things that seemed eerily similar to what you experience when you are awake. You're most likely not in a dream (or else this book is all your own thoughts instead of mine), but *proving* that you're not in a dream is more difficult than simply declaring it. There are, however, some indicators that you are not dreaming. For example, "real life" has a history. You can remember how you got to where you are right now. Dreams, on the other hand, just sort of happen; you can't recall how you ended up where you are in a dream.

My purpose in beginning this chapter by talking about dreams is to make the point that there are some things that are very difficult to *prove*, though you would swear that you absolutely knew them. This problem is magnified by the fact that all of our experiences must go through our mind, and our mind often lies to us.

Note: One quick clarifier that needs to be mentioned before we go on. In philosophy, the words mind *and* brain *do not refer to the same thing. One's mind is an indefinite descriptor for our cognitive faculties. A mind is not necessarily physical. A brain, on the other hand, is the three pounds of grey matter that exists between your ears. It is physical. We will address this difference in a later chapter, but for the purpose of this chapter, I will use these terms interchangeably, though there is a technical difference.*

How do you know that you're not just a brain in a vat and that all your experiences (that you think are real) are only in your mind? Imagine for a moment that you are indeed a brain in a scientific vat that keeps the brain alive. A mad scientist has inserted electrodes into your brain. By simply shocking the brain at certain locations, the scientist can make you experience what you think is "real life." You think you have a body, but that is just because the scientist has shocked the part of your brain that makes you experience what you think to be your body. You think you are holding this book in your hand, but actually, it is the scientist who is shocking another part of your brain to make you think you are holding the book in your hand. You are merely a brain in a laboratory jar, but like the movie *The Matrix*, everything you think is "real" *is only going on in your head.* The food you think you taste, the sights you think you see, and the sensations you think you feel all occur in your brain, so how do you know that you are not solely a brain?

Or what about other people? Do they exist in reality or just in your mind? After all, you have encountered other people in your dreams (that you thought were real), but they were nothing more than images you conjured up while dreaming. If you are a brain in a vat, then perhaps no one else but you (and maybe the mad scientist) exists. This is the problem of solipsism or the belief that you do not know that other minds/people exist. If all your thoughts occur in your mind, then all of the people you think you see could *solely* be in your mind. If all of your thoughts occur in your mind, then how do you get beyond your mind to the "real world"? Maybe you're the only person that really exists and everyone else is a figment of your imagination. As I once heard a philosophy professor joke, "I once knew a guy who was a solipsist. We always wanted to make sure he stayed alive because we knew that if he died, we would all die as well."

To be fair, most normal people don't actually think they are in the Matrix or just a brain in a vat. That would be silly. But here is the kicker (and why philosophy is so fun): *it is almost impossible to prove that you are not just a brain in a vat.* You would think that it would be really easy to prove that you really have a body and are really experiencing an external world. But it is notoriously difficult to prove, because everything that you think you are experiencing is being experienced in your mind and therefore could (technically) be occurring *only* in your mind.

With this scary fact in front of us, is there any knowledge we can have with certainty? Or are we doomed to skepticism and the inability to prove what we think we know?

Can we know anything with certainty?

If even the existence of the external world can be doubted, is there anything we can know for sure? René Descartes (1596–1650) (along with Francis Bacon) began what is known as the early modern era of philosophy. It is Descartes, in particular, who addressed this question. Descartes came up with a thought experiment to see if there is anything that we can know with absolute certainty—anything that cannot be doubted. For if there is anything we can indeed know with certainty, that thing could then become the foundation on which other areas of knowledge could be build.

To start, we must get rid of any beliefs that could possibly be wrong. We must try to doubt everything that can possibly be doubted. We must doubt that we are awake right now. We must doubt that our eyes are reliable. We must doubt that there is an external world. We must doubt that our memories are real (and were not implanted there by our mad scientist friend mentioned above). We certainly must doubt all of our sense perception (for we have all seen optical illusions and been tricked by our senses).

As a clarifier, Descartes is not saying that we are actually wrong on all these beliefs. He is simply conducting a thought experiment. He is saying that if anything we think we know can be doubted at all, then we must play devil's advocate and assume that it is wrong for now. Second, just to make the problem even worse, Descartes encourages us to imagine that there is an evil demon, and evil genius, or evil God who is actively trying to deceive us at every point. In addition to doubting everything that can be doubted, there is also an all-powerful being who is doing everything is his power to trick you. With the deck stacked against us in the worst way possible, is there anything we can know with certainty—is there anything about which we cannot be wrong?

This is where Descartes comes up with his famous answer: the one thing that I can't be wrong about is the fact that I am thinking. Even if I'm thinking wrong things or even if I'm being tricked, I'm still thinking. Even if an evil demon is tricking me into thinking wrong thoughts, I'm still thinking thoughts. *Cogito ergo sum* (I think, therefore I am). Descartes uses this insight as a foundation from which he goes on to prove many other things. From this simple axiom (which cannot be doubted) he tries to show that he knows he exists as a thinking thing, that God exists (since he has a conception of infinity, which he could get only from a God who is infinite, since we don't ever experience anything infinite); and since God is not a deceiver, Descartes also believes we can believe other things we think we know.

Descartes was preceded in this proof for absolute truth by the philosopher St. Augustine, who proved that the claim "I exist" must be absolutely true. This is because one who says "I exist" is either right (and therefore does indeed exist) or he is wrong (and therefore still exists, because a non-existing thing can't be wrong). After all, if one is deceived or wrong, *then they can't not exist.*

Now, don't worry about Descartes's grand conclusions about God and infinity and the external world just yet. We will talk more about potential proofs and potential refutations for God's existence in a later chapter. Let's back up a second and see if Descartes is right. Is it true that Descartes has come up with an irrefutable truth? On the one hand, Descartes's proof seems to be impenetrable. Even if there is an evil demon tricking me, then there still must be someone to trick. Even if I'm thinking wrong thoughts, I am still a thinking thing. But on the other hand, does Descartes prove that he exists *as a thinking thing* or merely, as Bertrand Russell would later claim about his argument, that *there is merely thinking* going on but no proof that Descartes is a thinking *thing*? Does Descartes prove that there is a "self" behind the thinking or just that thinking is happening? Descartes would probably say to Russell that the "self" is implied; after all, Descartes proves that there is thinking going on but immediately goes on to define himself as a "thinking thing."

Regardless of whether or not Descartes has proved the existence of an enduring self, he certainly has shown that there is one absolute truth we can hold (which cannot be wrong), and that is: there is indeed thinking when one claims that they think.

What do you think about Descartes's argument so far? Can Descartes imply all the things he does from the mere fact that his existence is certain when he claims to think? Does Descartes make the standard of knowledge too high? Do we first have to know something with absolute, unbreakable certainty before we can say we know other things? Can't I truly know my name is Zach without having to pretend that demons are tricking me and creating an absolute foundation of the mind and God first? Surely I know that there is a computer in front of me as I type this sentence, right?

Philosophers wrestle with Descartes's conclusions to this day. Some think his standard can be refuted. Most think his standard is unbreakable. Still others think his standard is true but feel as though it sets the bar far too high for future claims about knowledge. After all, can't we just trust our senses?

The problem with sense perception

If you ask the average American to list the things they believe in, they will likely point to things known to us through sense perception. They believe in things they think they can see, taste, hear, smell, and touch. This view, though commendable because of its simplicity, is a bit naïve. But why is it naïve? Why can't we just trust our senses?

Fist, as we showed in the chapter on metaphysics, there could be a whole host of things that exist that cannot be perceived by things such as sight and taste (God, numbers, concepts, relations, love, and theoretical entities such as quarks or tectonic plates). *But, more obviously, our senses lie to us all the time.* Stick a ruler into a glass of water, and the ruler looks bent. Draw two dots of the same size, and then draw a large circle around one and a small circle around the other, and the dots no longer look like they are the same size. Simply google "optical illusions" and rest assured that your senses are constantly lying to you.

Your eyes are not trustworthy. Look at a chair, and it looks one size, but then back away, and it looks smaller. Stars seem to "twinkle" though they are not actually turning on and off really quickly. In fact, every time you've seen a magician do a "magic trick" your senses have lied to you. Optical illusions, dreams, the fact that our taste changes when we are sick, a body part going numb, an amputee "feeling" a lost limb, and a million other examples could be given for why you should not trust your senses. Someone who has a brain tumor may even "smell" a burning odor, though nothing is actually burning. Your senses are not bad. We couldn't survive without them. *But they do not give you an adequate and unfailing picture of the world and therefore cannot be fully trusted.* This is why so many philosophers, like Descartes, are trying to get you to trust unfailing logic over failing senses.

But trying to use only your senses to understand the external world runs you into even trickier problems. Now, bear with me on this paragraph, because if you understand what I'm saying it will blow your mind: you never actually experience an object directly with your senses. *Rather, you experience your experience of the object.* That sounds a bit abstract, so allow me to give a few examples. When I touch a tree with my hand, I don't actually experience the tree itself (apart from the sensation in my hand). *I experience my experience of the tree.* This is for the simple reason that the nerve endings in my hands don't extend down into the wood of the tree; they extend only to the end of my hand. *What I'm feeling when I press my hand against the tree is not the tree itself but rather . . . my hand. All my experiences are skin-in.* I'm not saying that a tree is not somehow related to me feeling sensations in my hand. A tree is, indeed, interacting with my hand. But I don't experience the "feeling" of the tree. *I experience (in my mind) the sensations I get from the nerve endings in my hand (none of which are in the tree).*

Perhaps you have never considered this. When you feel pain in your hand (from touching a hot skillet), the place that is actually telling you that there is pain is not in your hand; it is in your head. Yet, you don't feel the pain in your brain (where the very source of pain neurons exist). Rather, you feel the pain in your hand. If you were to apply a narcotic to make your hand go numb, you wouldn't feel anything at all (despite the fact that your hand was still being burned).

When I use my eyes to see a table from across the room, I'm not actually seeing the table directly. The image is going to my eyes and then being interpreted by my brain. This means that, though I believe the table is really there, I'm not experiencing the table in some absolute, objective way. *I have access to the image of the table only in my mind.* I have access only to the *idea* of a table. In fact, the table changes as I move across the room. The size of the table changes as I get further away, and the color of the table changes as the light reflects differently off of it (based upon my viewing angle). I'm not objectively experiencing the table (or else the size and color wouldn't be changing as I move). *Rather, I'm experiencing the image of the table that is in my mind.*

As I get closer to the table, it looks bigger. As I back away, the table looks smaller. The table is not changing, but my image of the table that I'm experiencing only in my mind (for where else could I even experience it?) continues to change. Light is bouncing off of the table, traveling across the room into my eyes, and then being interpreted by my brain. *But I can experience only the table that is being perceived by my senses and interpreted by my mind and not the table itself (apart from my senses interpreted by my mind).* I can interact only with my thought table, not an objective table detached from my thoughts. I cannot interact with the table without going through the *medium of my ideas.* All the experiences of the table that I have don't come merely from my nerve endings; they come from my senses *as they are understood by my mind.* A dead person could be in a room with a table, but they wouldn't experience a table at all because their mind cannot perceive it.

Another reason we cannot trust our senses is because the outside object we are trying to perceive may be objectively different from how we subjectively perceive it. How do I know that the perceived table in my mind is *exactly* the same as the table is in reality when no one is perceiving it?

John Locke distinguished between what he called primary, secondary, and tertiary qualities. These have to do with which qualities are in an object itself and which qualities are in us and our perceptions. There may be some qualities that a table possesses in and of itself (that are actually in the table) such as extension. But there are other qualities that are not in the object itself but rather in us. Color is one of his examples. When I see a red shirt, the "color" is not in the shirt. The color is in me; it is in my mind. The light bounces off of the shirt, goes into my eye, and my mind perceives color. *But the color is not in the shirt, or else there would be a big streak of red in the air in between the shirt and my eye.* To prove the point, a color-blind person sees the shirt as a different color than I because the perception of color is in him, not the shirt. However, notice that the color-blind person doesn't see the shirt as a different shape. The shape of the shirt is different than the color of the shirt. The shape of the shirt is in the shirt, but the color is in us.

We don't technically see with our eyes; we see with our mind. Consider someone who is hallucinating. They "see" things that aren't really there, and they "see" them with just as much vivacity as they do objects that are really there. This is because the mind is where the rubber meets the road. Regardless of what light and images go through your eyes, it is the mind that must interpret them.

To give another Lockean example, when we put our hand close to a fire we say that there is "heat" in the fire because we feel heat with our hand. But if we put our hand even closer to the fire, it causes pain. But we don't say that there is "pain" in the fire. Rather, the pain is in us. Why then did we say that "heat" was in the fire but we didn't say that "pain" was in the fire *when we felt both of them in the exact same way?* The fire causes us to sense certain things in us—not in the actual object. Some of the qualities are in the object itself (primary qualities) and others are in us. To be clear, the fire does objectively warm up the air around us (I'm not denying that fire produces heat). Locke's point, rather, is that we must epistemologically distinguish qualities in an object from qualities that are in us.

To be clear, this does not mean that the objects outside of us—the shirt or fire in these examples—do *nothing* to cause secondary qualities to be perceived by us. They certainly do. But the way an object has extension is quite different than the way it causes us to see color.

Is Locke right? How do we know that the table itself (with its primary qualities) exists in the object and are not merely assumed? Don't we perceive the table's extension in a way similar to how we perceive its color? Perhaps all of the properties are dependent on our mind. This is the view of a philosopher we will meet later in the book who believes Locke was being arbitrary. *Maybe all the things we see are ideas in the mind, and nothing is an unperceived material substance.* Maybe all qualities are in the mind.

One more quick thing to note. We do not experience a "substance"; we experience only "properties." If you think back to our chapter on metaphysics, a substance is what something really is. It is the underlying thing that remains and defines a thing, even though that thing's accidental properties may change. A dog, Fido, is a substance, and the fact that it is white is merely a property. But here is what is tricky: How do we actually know that substances exist? *We don't seem to experience substance.* When I see a horse, I don't see its underlying form of "horse-ness." Rather, I experience merely its properties. I see the color brown, I see that it is solid, I see that it is tall, I hear it make that weird sound horses make. But I don't actually experience the substance: horse. I perceive merely a bundle of properties. But surely there has to be a substance of *horse*, right? I can't just take the color brown, a fur blanket, and an audio recording of a horse whinnying and throw them together and assume that I've created a horse. There must be something that stands under (again, hence the name *sub-stance*) these properties that makes a thing what it is.

But how do we know that? Our chapter on metaphysics asked questions like "What makes a horse a horse?" This chapter is a little different in that it asks, "How do we know that a horse is even a substance at all if all we experience through our senses are properties?" Epistemology deals with what we can know and how we know it. Though we are apt to trust just our senses, our experiences can be deceiving. This leads to another interesting debate in the study of knowledge, and that is the question of whether or not all of our knowledge comes from experience.

Rationalism vs. empiricism

Do we know things only after having an experience (a posteriori) or do we have some type of knowledge (possibly innate) that is known without (or before) experience (a priori)? *Is our knowledge gained merely by experience, or is some of our knowledge known without experience?* This is the main question in the rationalism versus empiricism debate. Some, like George Berkeley, David Hume, and John Locke, believed that experience is the mode, par excellence, for how we come to know things. Locke described our minds as a blank slate (a *tabula rasa*). We don't have knowledge until we experience things. We know things only after we have experiences and we can mix and match experiences to create new thoughts.

Others, such as René Descartes, Benedict Spinoza, Gottfried Leibniz, and even some of their predecessors, such as Plato, believed that we have knowledge that is not derived from experience. When it comes to epistemology, the rationalists put a premium on the ability of reason, instead of experience, to obtain knowledge. *The rationalists are not saying that we don't receive any knowledge from experience.* They believe we actually receive a lot of info from experience. They just think that some of our most basic (and most important) beliefs are not acquired through experience.

Which view do you think is correct? Most Americans, because of the scientific and pragmatic presuppositions of our culture, tend to be empiricists. We tend to think that a newborn baby is basically an epistemological chalkboard. When the baby sees a flower, for example, we assume that an image is etched onto their mental chalkboard of a flower. That seems pretty straightforward. However, as you may have already guessed, nothing in philosophy is that simple. The rationalist will point to several examples to show why all our knowledge can't be based on experience.

First, if we are just a *tabula rasa* or blank slate, how can we receive even the first impression of something we experience? Wouldn't you need some type of "grid" to which that first image could attach? Consider again our example of the baby that first sees a flower. How does that flower image "stick" in the baby's mind if the baby doesn't have any preformed categories of knowledge onto which the image can "stick"? In the same way that Velcro doesn't stick very well to a cue ball, so the things we experience would need some type of mental Velcro to which they can attach. Additionally, the baby seems to know some things innately. For example, the baby knows how to suck for milk and how to cry when it needs something, and has an innate *ability to learn language* as it grows (though it wasn't taught how to do these things). These three examples won't win over the most hardened empiricist (as many empiricists believe in things such as instinct), but the rationalist has a whole arsenal of stronger examples.

We have, as Descartes had mentioned, a concept of infinity. Yet—and this is fascinating—*we have never experienced anything infinite through our senses*. From where then does this concept arise? You may be tempted to say that our concept of infinity actually does come from experience. Perhaps we start counting individual objects, say, sticks on the ground, and just imagine what it would be like to count them forever. We conjecture what it would be like if the numbers just kept going up. But if you think about the problem this way, you've made a logical mistake.

First, you haven't actually experienced infinity. You have just experienced one stick, and then a second stick, and then a third stick, etc. *But— and follow me closely here—the idea of counting them forever was already in your head.* As soon as you counted a few sticks and then jumped to the conclusion that the number could just keep on going up, that "forever-ness" was already a concept in your mind. To summarize this notion in a way I once heard a professor quip in a lecture: when you think of infinity you think of the number one, and then the number two, and then the number three, and then you think of the numbers continuing to go up. You think of the idea of "one, two, three . . ." But what on earth does ". . ." mean? What is it that the ellipsis stands for? In fact, it is the concept of infinity that you have already assumed. You are arguing in a circle. You began thinking that counting could go on into infinity and then, after counting a few sticks, assumed that it could go on to infinity. The rationalist will show that the concept of "forever" or "infinite" was already in your mind. You didn't get it from experience. It was already in you.

Or consider the idea of substance. Remember, a substance for Aristotle is an underlying individual object. But, as we saw earlier, we experience only properties—not the substance itself. So how can it be that we all assume that an individual human is an actual thing (an actual substance) and not just a collection of hair color, height, and solidity? We all agree that a person is the same person throughout their life even though their weight or hair color changes. The rationalist will say that the concept of substance was already in our mind. We don't ever actually experience the substance unmediated by properties, and yet, it seems to be something we know without experience.

Additionally, *inferences* from experience (not just the experience itself) are things we don't gain through experience. We may experience a physical object, for example, but the inferences we draw from that thing seem to be an innate type of knowledge. How am I able to see a flower and see a campfire and then come up with the idea that the fire will burn the flower if I've never seen that event occur?

Or consider the law of noncontradiction. This logical axiom is not something that we gain from experience. All propositions (statements that claim something) are either true or false—a thing can either be or not be— *but a statement cannot be both true and false in the exact same way at the same time, and a thing cannot both be and not be in the same way at the same time.* But the truth of this statement is not something we experience. If it is indeed sunny outside right now and I say "It is sunny outside right now," we inherently see that this statement is true, and its contradiction, "It is not sunny outside right now," is false. *But this obviously logical truth is not something we experienced.* Of course we experienced the day being sunny, but the truthfulness of the law of noncontradiction we didn't experience. *In fact, this logical law seems to be something that we have to already know in order to have even our first experience.*

Is the rationalist right? Or is this all some sort of Jedi mind trick? Do you think we have innate knowledge, or should we be looking to experience alone as the source for the things we know? What comes hardwired into our minds (or perhaps placed there by God) so that we can know other things? Or is it the case that nothing is hardwired until after one has an experience? There is no easy answer. The empiricists have answers to each of these arguments, and the rationalists have counterarguments. But one of the members in the empiricist party shows how strict empiricism can lead to some pretty scary extremes.

David Hume and causation

The happy skeptic, David Hume, was like an atomic bomb that fell on the playground of epistemology. It's not an exaggeration to say that he basically destroyed everything we thought we knew up until that time (which means he was also a pretty sharp philosopher). He categorized all of our knowledge into two types; this division is called *Hume's fork* because it has two "prongs." The first is what are called *relations of ideas.* This has to do with how ideas relate to each other, deductively, in our mind. The idea that two plus two equals four or that all bachelors are unmarried are relations of ideas. These are analytic statements—statements that are true by definition. These ideas are important, but they have very little to do with our day-to-day lives. They also *may* be derived from experience (depending on which philosopher you ask).

Almost all of our knowledge actually comes from the second category—what Hume calls *matters of fact.* This is the second "prong" of Hume's fork. Relations of ideas and matters of fact are the only two ways of knowing for Hume. Here is where Hume becomes the bad guy: *our knowledge of matters of fact (which are most of the things we think we know) is based on things we can't actually experience.* Specifically, almost all of our knowledge of the world is based on the concept of causation, *but we never actually experience causation.* When one billiard ball hits another billiard ball, we see the first ball move and stop and then the second ball move and stop. But we don't actually *experience* the "cause." That cause is something we infer. It is something we assume. All we actually experience is one ball moving and another ball moving. When you say "That's silly, of course the first billiard ball caused the second one to move," you are merely assuming that there is a cause, but you cannot actually prove that *through experience alone.* You can see a ball. A ball has color and shape. But you can't see a cause. What color is a cause? How much does a cause weight? What shape is a cause? Causation is something that we infer. It is not something that we experience directly (like the actual billiard balls). But on what do we base this inference, since it can't be on sense perception?

To give a strange example, imagine that a baby, as soon as it is born, is placed in a room by itself until it grows up. The baby is suspended in the air, and medical tubes are used to feed the baby until it becomes an adult. The baby has no interaction with anyone and never sees any physical objects other than the feeding tubes and the room. As soon as the baby is an adult and has had almost no experiences, someone brings a pool table into the room and hits one billiard ball toward another billiard ball. What would the baby (now adult) think that the cue ball would do when it hits another ball? *The answer is that the adult would have no idea.* The adult would see that one ball moved another ball, but the idea of one "causing" the other to move would be totally foreign to this person who grew up without experiences. Perhaps he thinks the ball will stop. Perhaps he thinks the ball will explode. Perhaps he thinks the whole table will disappear. He would have no idea what would happen, because causation cannot be experienced through the senses. The adult could see one ball move and then another ball move, but he would never see "causation." Causation is not a sensed concept and so, by definition, cannot be experienced.

To summarize: since Hume is an empiricist, he believes that all of our practical knowledge must be based on experience. However, we cannot experience one of the most important things we need to have knowledge, and that is causation.

Hume believes that our supposed "knowledge" of matters of fact and causation is actually not knowledge at all. Rather, we trick ourselves into believing that we have knowledge when we don't. All we actually have is constant conjunction. We just have one event that follows in time from another event, and we assume that one "causes" the other when really all we have observed are two events separated by a small amount of time. What does this mean? Let me ask it this way: Do you believe that the sun will rise tomorrow? You will probably say yes. Why do you think the sun will rise tomorrow? You will probably say something like "Because, in my past experiences, the sun rises each day." But notice what mistake you are making by using this line of reasoning. Just because the sun rose in the past gives you *absolutely no reason* to believe that it will rise in the future. Just because something in the past has happened one way, there is no reason to think that it will be like that in the future. I may assume that I will live tomorrow just because I have lived for many days up until now, but on the day of my death, my presupposition will be false.

Hume believes that all of our knowledge is just habit (constant conjunction) and we have no reason to think that we know the things we think we know. Imagine a child goes to open their refrigerator door, and as they do, someone happens to ring their doorbell at the same time. The child closes the door again and, while looking puzzled, begins to open the refrigerator door a second time to see what happens. By chance, the person waiting at the door has become impatient and rings the doorbell at the exact same time the child opens the refrigerator door for the second time. The child may assume that when they open the refrigerator door, this causes the doorbell to ring. *But just because one event follows another in time (the doorbell ringing immediately follows the opening of the refrigerator door), opening the refrigerator door in no way causes the doorbell to ring.*

Hume believes that all our knowledge of causation is like this. Everything is like the refrigerator door and the doorbell example. Things follow one another in time and we mis-infer that one causes the other. But we don't actually experience the causation; we have merely created a habit, and we assume that this habit is actual knowledge. I think the sun will rise tomorrow or that one ball causes another ball to move only because I have seen a constant conjunction or habit of the sun rising and billiard balls striking others—not because I can experience causation.

Immanuel Kant

The response to Hume is devised by a man who is probably in the top three or four most influential philosophers in world history. His name is Immanuel Kant. Kant's work (like Hegel, Heidegger, and others) is very difficult to understand, and scholars who have spent their entire lives studying him disagree with one another on exactly what he means at several places of his famous three-volume critique: the *Critique of Pure Reason* on metaphysics and epistemology, the *Critique of Practical Reason* on ethics, and the *Critique of Judgment* on aesthetics and teleology. We will not be able, in this short volume, to fully dive into such a deep and complicated thinker. (The most difficult class I ever took was a doctoral seminar in Kant, and I'm still reeling from it today.) Suffice it to say that what Kant will do is to give an answer to Hume but in a way that will change philosophy forever. Let's take a look at how he does this.

For most (but not all) of Western history some people assumed that the mind's job was not to form the world but rather to be passive. By "passive" I don't mean that the mind isn't working hard. Rather, I mean that the mind's job was figuring out what was "out there" in the external world. The mind was like a piece of wax, and when we experienced something, such as a key, the key was pressed into the wax, thus creating the idea of a key. Hume destroyed all of that.

The way to refute Hume is by showing that the mind actively structures the world. For Kant there are indeed real objects (what he calls *noumena*—which are things as they are in themselves). But, for Kant, we cannot get to the noumena. Rather, we can experience only the *phenomena*, which is a combination of the object itself with how it is perceived by our minds, which actively structure the world. We don't perceive the object all by itself. We perceive the object only after it has been predigested by our mind's active structuring of the world.

If that sounds complex, it is. Let me say it in a less complicated way. Our minds don't just passively perceive objects but are involved in laying certain cognitive structures (for Kant these are the structures of space and time and twelve philosophical categories, which include things like substance) onto our experience. Our minds provide an objective and universal set of cognitive structures onto the world that is outside of us. If you didn't get all that, the big point that you need to take away is that, from Kant onward, philosophers would realize more and more the infinite gulf between an object as it is in itself and an object as it is predigested by the cognitive structures of our mind. To be clear, our mind doesn't create reality. But we can't ever take off our Kantian mind glasses to see the way the world "really is." Our minds actively structure the world. Since our minds lay a grid of space and time onto the noumena, this is how we can understand causation and thus defeat Hume.

Furthermore, before Kant many people basically thought that there was knowledge gained from experience (a posteriori) and possibly knowledge one had before (or without) experience (a priori). Knowledge gained by experience was something like "a mean dog will bite you." Knowledge not gained by experience was something like "five plus four equals nine." If these are the only two ways of knowing, then Hume has trapped us. These are the famous two prongs of his fork (relations of ideas and matters of fact).

For Hume, some things were analytic and understood by definition (such as two plus two equals four). These things were known a priori. Other things were synthetic and understood from experience (such as the sky being blue). These things were known a posteriori. However, Kant believed that there was a third category of knowledge called *synthetic a priori knowledge*—meaning, he thought that there was a category that Hume missed. Perhaps something could be known without experience (hence "a priori") but could also give us new knowledge in the conclusion that is not contained in the premise (hence "synthetic").

For Kant, our knowledge of things that seem certain (even mathematics) is not necessarily analytic. (By analytic he means that they seem to be tautological—the information in the conclusion seems to be the same as the information in the premise.) For example, five plus four (which equals nine) equals nine. So when we do a math problem (such as this one) really all we are saying is that nine equals nine. This statement would be something that is analytic; there is no new information in the conclusion that is not in the premise. But Kant pointed out that we have made a mistake here. There is nothing about the number five, the concept of plus, the second number four, and the concept of an equals sign that actually leads to nine. You don't get "nine" from just observing the following things: plus-ness, five, four, math, etc. This means that even statements from mathematics can give us new (synthetic) knowledge. After all, if math were only analytic, then we would expect math students to never get an equation wrong on a math test!

Don't freak out if you didn't understand this last part. Kant is a tricky philosopher to understand. What you should be wrestling with are questions like: Is all knowledge derived from experience or not? If it is all from experience, then what about things I can't experience with my senses like causation? Are our minds passive and merely receive the information out in the world, or do they help construct the world? If my mind structures the world, how will I ever know what an object is apart from my mind (what the object is in and of itself)?

Justified true belief

Throughout much of the history of philosophy, knowledge has been defined as "justified true belief." Each of the three parts of this definition are really important. First, to really have knowledge, your thoughts about something must be *justified*—meaning, you need to be able to give reasons for why you think that something is correct instead of accidentally being correct. Imagine that your favorite number just happens to be 180. During a geometry quiz the test asks you how many degrees are in a triangle. You don't know the answer, but you just put down 180 because that's your favorite number. Your answer is correct. But you got it right only on a guess. Your belief was not based on the fact that you took out your protractor and measured all the angles or that you remembered some mathematical proof. A guess can't be true "knowledge." For something to be *knowledge*, it must be justified. You must have good reasons for why you know what you think you know.

Additionally, for something to be knowledge, it has to be true. If something is false, then it is obviously not knowledge. If you believe that two plus two equals five and even try to give some justification for why you came to that conclusion, you still don't have true knowledge, because false knowledge is not actually knowledge. If you believe that Santa exists when—spoiler alert—he doesn't exist, then that obviously cannot be considered knowledge.

Lastly, you have to believe something for it to be knowledge. If dinosaurs once roamed the earth, but you don't believe that dinosaurs ever existed, then, in addition to needing to visit a museum, you would also not have true knowledge. If something is justified and true, then there is no reason you should not believe it. And it is only when you have all three of these components that you have knowledge.

What do you think of this definition of knowledge so far? Do you agree with it? It seems to be watertight, but it is not without its critics.

Many have wondered if this definition of knowledge is correct. How justified does something have to be before it can be knowledge? If someone believes that the Virgin Mary came to them in a dream and then becomes a fervent Roman Catholic because of that experience, is that knowledge? One could make a case for that idea. They might say that it is justified (since the reason the person became a Catholic was due to a powerful Catholic experience), that it is true (if indeed one thinks the beliefs of the Catholic church are factual), and that it is belief (as, obviously, this example deals explicitly with believing something). But most people would not consider this knowledge. After all, it being justified and true are strongly in question. How strongly do you have to believe something for you to *know* it?

Consider a reworking of what is known as the *Gettier problem*, which is a critique of defining knowledge as justified true belief. Pretend I have been told by my boss that someone I really like will be getting a promotion. I ask who it is, and my boss, with a smile, says that it is someone who works in my department and whose car has a flat tire. I assume he is talking about my buddy, Mike. Mike works in my department, and I saw that his car had a flat tire at lunch. I then formulate the idea that "someone who works in my department, whom I like, who had a flat tire, will get the promotion." However, it turns out that Mike doesn't get the promotion, but I do get the promotion. And, interestingly, I happen to meet all of these criteria: I'm someone I like. I'm someone who works in my department. And, as I leave the office excited about getting the promotion, I realize that my car has a flat tire that my boss must have seen earlier in the day. I believed something (hence belief), it was true (someone with a flat tire did get a promotion), and I had justified reasons for believing it (my boss had told me that someone in my department with a flat tire would get the promotion). But did I truly have knowledge in this instance? Something seems to have gone seriously wrong.

Do problems like this, originally posed in a different form by Edmund Gettier, defeat the definition of knowledge as justified true belief or not? Was my knowledge really justified if things happen to turn out the way I thought but in a different way than I thought they would? Is the definition of knowledge as justified true belief a good one, or do we need to add some qualifiers? What qualifiers would you add? If you think it is a good definition, how would you answer the Gettier problem?

Degrees of certainty

Before finishing our chapter, it would be prudent to discuss the fact that there are different degrees of how certain we can be regarding any particular thing we think we know.

Consider how certain you are of each of the following propositions:

1. You are not in a dream right now.

2. A square has four sides.

3. Archangels exist.

4. Columbus discovered America.

Each of these propositions could be considered claims of knowledge, even the ones we are not certain are true. Some of them seem very certain, such as number 2. Others seem pretty certain (but not absolute), such as number 1. Number 3 will vary in certainty depending on what you think about theological and religious topics. Number 4 may be correct, but it does depend on whose history book you are reading.

The point is that, when it comes to a theory of knowledge, we need to know that knowledge can be had in degrees. Some things you will know with much more force than other things. The knowledge that I exist seems pretty high. The knowledge I have of what I think the stock market will do tomorrow is less so.

How certain do you have to be before you can truly have "knowledge"? If you are a Muslim, do you *know* that God exists? How sure are you? Or, if you are an atheist, do you *know* that God doesn't exist? How sure are you? Most discussions of epistemology don't do an adequate job of clarifying just how sure is sure enough. We saw that there are those, like Descartes, who have a very high degree of certainty. But is his bar too high? Can't I know that I had cereal for breakfast without having to formulate a logical proof?

Conclusion

Epistemology is one of the most important areas of philosophy. After all, to have knowledge of any other area of philosophy, you need to know what counts as knowledge. People make claims every day for what they think they know. They know it is raining, they know their business will fail, they know where they live. However, if you press them on how they know each of these things, their answers become a bit tenuous.

Perhaps one of the most offensive things new students of philosophy have to stomach is the cold, hard truth that *you don't have a right to believe what you think without evidence. You have a right to hold only positions for which you can argue.* You have a right to hold only what you can defend. Simply holding a view without evidence is literally how superstition and ignorance flourish.

In addition to the fancy term *epistemology,* knowledge has another term that is often used in a modern context. It is the very familiar word *science.* This word comes from a Latin word pertaining to knowledge, *scientia.* And it is this topic that will be addressed in our next chapter.

Science

MANY OLDER INTRODUCTIONS TO philosophy do not have a section on the philosophy of science. In fact, what we think of as "natural science" was not its own, separate branch of knowledge for most of Western history. Aristotle was as comfortable observing the growing habits of plants (biology) as he was talking about "being" (metaphysics). However, since it is now a distinct discipline (and because it is so familiar to our culture) it has become necessary for philosophers to open a portal to an entire "philosophy of science."

There is no doubt that modern science is an incredible benefit to humanity. This morning, I woke up because an electric alarm clock kept time for me. My house was kept cool because of air conditioning. I got in a car, rather than rode a horse, to work. I didn't die from measles, because I was vaccinated against it as a child. I visited with a friend who flew, on a magic, metal bird called an "airplane"; he traveled a distance that used to take months in just a few hours. I can pick up a small rectangle from my pocket and look up almost any piece of information in the world. I can record a song, buy a car, have a package delivered the same day, or even take part in a video call with someone on the other side of the world—all in a few seconds. If I get sick, medicine will make me better. If I need a new heart, I can have one transplanted. Surgeries are no longer performed by hacking off a limb while biting down on a leather belt after drinking whiskey; we now have anesthesia. Surgeries may take only minutes, and they are performed by robotics.

Every area of our lives is so impacted by science that it is impossible to think of how society would look today if we still went to witch doctors when we felt ill or sacrificed animals to make the crops grow. Someone in the eighteenth century had more in common with those of ancient Samaria than with us. We should all be very thankful for the findings of modern science.

The reason I'm beginning this chapter by praising the advances of modern science is because I don't want anyone to critique me for being unscientific or "anti-science." The goal of a philosopher is to question everything, and this includes even the helpful field of science. I tip my hat to the men and women who work hard to make our lives better through science and technology. But as a philosopher, I have to point out that science is not perfect. It is a tool but an evolving and correctible one.

As incredible as science is, there are two assumptions, held by most people in the twenty-first century, that need to be dispelled. The first is that science is purely objective and is not influenced by any theories, biases, or agendas. The second is that the way we perceive the world today (a world of atoms, magnetic fields, and black holes) is exactly like scientists tell us it is. Let us begin with the first of these assumptions by stating a shocking but incredibly true claim: science is not objective.

Science is not objective

This sentence sounds like something only a neanderthal would say. It sounds like something said by a flat-earther or science denier. Isn't the very reason so many people trust science is because it is objective? Isn't science the one thing that we can really "hang our hat on" when we want to understand the world around us?

It may surprise you to find out that what I've just said—"science is not objective"—is readily acknowledged by most scientists and philosophers of science. *This does not mean that science is not true or that it does not work.* Science works great! Rather, it is to point out that there are no theory-independent notions of how we come to know things. *There is no science that doesn't depend on a philosophical foundation.* Science, since it studies what we think we know, is actually a subset of epistemology, and as we saw earlier, epistemology is anything but simple. When we are looking for "objective truth," we by definition are doing philosophy, not science. To further make this point. Let's look at a few examples of why science cannot be completely objective.

First, science must presuppose certain things before it can even begin; it rests on philosophical presuppositions. Let's take, for example, a central claim of the scientific method. Consider the statement: "Science finds truth based on what is perceived through one of the five senses." Pause for a second and ask yourself, "Why do we think that sentence is true?" In fact, the sentence "Science finds truth based on what is perceived through one of the five senses" *is not itself provable through one of the five senses*! It is a logical proposition that has no taste or smell. *We didn't come up with the scientific method by using the scientific method.* This sentence is a claim from philosophy that didn't (itself) use the scientific method. We came up with that notion of empiricism based on philosophy and not by running that sentence through the machine of the scientific method. We cannot even begin doing science until we have used philosophy as a type of foundation.

Many of us begin with a rather naïve notion, learned from our science teachers in elementary school, that there is an objective scientific method (only one!), and if we just follow this method, we will get an unbiased, assumption-less, theory-independent fact of the world without any of our preset assumptions tainting the results. Not only are there different variants of the scientific method, but they are anything but assumption-less.

For example, let's say we want to figure out whether or not smoking cigarettes causes lung cancer. That sounds simple enough. We just do medical check-ups with people who smoke and people who don't smoke to see the results, right?

Wrong! Think of all of presuppositions one must have to conduct even this simple experiment. Does the scientist work for a big tobacco company who wants the results to come back saying cigarettes are safe? In what way will he set up the experiments to prove his point? Does the scientist work for an organization who hates big tobacco companies and wants the results to come back saying cigarettes are dangerous? In what way will he set up the experiments to prove his point? What *type* of cigarettes should we study? Do we want to use the types with the most tobacco and no filters or the types with less tobacco and filters? Do we want to study young people who smoke or older people who smoke? Do we want to consider other health factors like the cancer history of someone's family before we study them? What about the patients who would have gotten lung cancer even if they didn't smoke and yet merely *happened* to smoke; did the cigarettes cause that cancer? Is our medical equipment able to do these tests perfectly, considering that technology is always getting better? On what basis will we choose the race of the patients? *How can we prove that there is causation and not just correlation?* Saying "smoking *causes* cancer" (think back to our friend, Hume, on causation) is a totally different claim than saying "people who smoked also *got* cancer." Or, and this is the most important question, *why did we even decide to do this experiment in the first place?* What practical considerations made us want to study cigarettes and lung cancer? Did we have a parent who smokes who we were trying to convince to quit? Did we have a big company we were trying to sue for damages? Why do we even care about this question? Notice, we didn't just start with lung cancer data. We made a decision to do this experiment instead of studying another topic (such as the mating habits of frogs) *because there was already something we wanted to prove.* Before we even began doing "science," we wanted to know the results of cigarette smoking for some purpose. And when we are talking about purpose, we are doing philosophy, not science.

There is no "doing science" without beginning assumptions that, themselves, are not based on science. To give a simpler example, imagine that a cosmologist (a scientist who studies the beginning of the universe) is an atheist. Before he has done even a single experiment, he has already concluded that there must be a naturalistic and materialistic cause of the universe (or that the universe is eternal) and has taken God out of the picture. He didn't prove that position via science. He started with this assumption even before doing the science. Or consider a cosmologist who is a devoted Muslim. Before he has done even a single experiment, he has already concluded that Allah must be the ultimate cause of the universe. He didn't prove that via science. He started with this assumption even before doing the science. There is no way to pursue any type of knowledge or data without presuppositions, and presuppositions are a category of philosophy.

Second, scientist disagree with each other. This fact should astound us. In every topic, from vaccine schedules for young kids to treatments for mental illness, doctors disagree with each other—*even when they are looking at the exact same data.* The very fact that people get a "second opinion" by an alternate doctor after receiving a cancer diagnosis is evidence that there is always the human element of interpretation. *Science is an art, not a science* (to turn a popular idiom on its head). Science, by its very nature, is meant to be challenged, changed, and tested.

What causes two scientists who graduated with the same grades from the same school to take entirely different approaches to, say, a global pandemic? We saw this with the advent of COVID-19. Conservative doctors and liberal doctors (some of whom studied at the exact same medical schools) came to radically different conclusions about the virus, despite the fact that they were looking at the same data and doing the same tests. The

CDC disagreed with health organizations in European countries, despite the fact that they are all run by scientists. Surely this shows that there are often strong assumptions in the background of the doctor's mind. Often, when there is an absolute scientific "consensus" being promoted by the scientific community, somebody is selling something. If all the doctors agreed on something, then they would all be out of a job, because there wouldn't be anything left to know on that topic. To say it more precisely, *science* doesn't say anything; only *scientists* say things. Science has no mouth, tongue, or vocal cords. Only fallible humans actually speak.

Third, science changes all the time. "Science" used to say the earth is flat. Now it says the earth is a sphere. Science used to say Newton's theories were correct. Now it says that Einstein's are better. Science used to say you should bleed someone who had a fever. Now it says you should just take Tylenol. *There is not one approved fact of science that has not been corrected by the science from a later era. As many philosophers of science have pointed out: the science of one generation is seen as the superstition of another.*

This change in science is not a bad thing. It is the nature of science to change previous beliefs when newer, better theories appear. *But it does mean that we must never put our full trust in a particular scientific theory.* Whatever the majority of scientists believe today is merely the most agreed-upon theory; it is not necessarily the right theory. If history has taught us anything, later scientists will make fun of how silly our beliefs about science were during our lifetime. What science needs is a big spoonful of humility. Scientists should be able to say what they think is the case without acting as though people are not allowed to challenge their thinking.

Fourth, science is only inductive and not deductive. Science is not like math. Math gives you absolute answers that don't change based on new factors. It doesn't matter how many times you try to solve the equation two plus two. The answer has always been four, the answer is currently four, and the answer will always be four. Science, on the other hand, doesn't have that same type of certainty; it gives you only degrees of probability. For example, I can look at one hundred swans and make the grand conclusion that "all swans are white." That conclusion is probable based on the information I currently have. However, that claim is only probable—not necessary. Black swans do indeed exist, which I failed to take into account in my sweeping (yet limited) conclusion. Induction is where you look at several individual cases and then surmise a larger conclusion. It therefore is only ever probable and not certain. Even if I search all the places that humans can go (the forest, the ocean, even the moon) the claim "unicorns don't exist" is only highly, highly probable but not certain. Since we haven't checked everywhere in the universe, we don't know this with certainly. There (logically) could be a unicorn in some other universe that we will never see. Though I certainly don't believe that unicorns exist anywhere, it is at least *logically possible* that there is a unicorn somewhere. Science deals only in probabilities, not certainties. Water always freezes at thirty-two degrees Fahrenheit, but there is nothing logically impossible about it freezing at another temperature.

Fifth, science contains elements of faith. To be clear, by faith, I don't mean religious faith. We will save that usage of the word *faith* for our chapter on religion. Rather, I mean it contains elements that one must take for granted before one begins. As soon as you look through a microscope, you are already assuming that the microscope will help you see small things. You didn't actually construct the microscope at the microscope factory (and therefore know what it will do with certainty) before you looked through it. You assumed it. You took it on faith when another scientist said, "Why don't you go over there and look through the microscope." Most of us have never actually seen germs with our eyes. They do exist, but we take other people's word for it. When a doctor prescribes medicine for us, we rarely know what it does, but we freely take what the doctor orders. Even as helpful as science is, it is not truly without some leaps in the dark. "Faith" is not just a religious thing. It is something we all have in areas where we have not personally ventured. In the same way that I have never seen Abraham Lincoln and must therefore trust that the historian is not lying to me, I have never seen a lot of things concluded in science and must therefore trust that the scientist is not lying to me. Though some scientists hate hearing that they have things they take on faith and beginning (unproved) assumptions, it is a claim that is blisteringly true.

Sixth, science is not unaffected by cultural bias. Scientists have preferences. Scientists exist within a particular culture. Scientists vote for certain candidates. Many times, scientists begin to skew the data because of larger cultural changes that are happening around them. One of the best examples of this is the history of the *Diagnostic and Statistical Manual of Mental Disorders* (DSM). This is the standard text that lists mental disorders for those who work in the fields of psychology and psychiatry. There have been many revisions to this work. Sometimes, disorders are added or removed because more research has been done in this field. Other times, "disorders" are added or removed because culture has changed its view on what it thinks is acceptable behavior. *Notice that, sometimes, what changes is not the science.* Rather, it is the culture around the scientist that has changed, and the *DSM* reflects that cultural change accordingly.

Seventh, and most importantly, science is founded on philosophical notions such as epistemology and metaphysics. For example, if one believes that everything is made of atoms, then that person is a monist. That is not just a scientific claim; it is a metaphysical claim. And the person making that claim, like our buddy, Heraclitus, thinks that the universe is made of only one thing. This leads to all the problems we saw in metaphysics earlier in the book. Or, as soon as one tries to take in knowledge solely through one's experience, they are playing in the realm of phenomenology and epistemology, thus leading back to philosophy. That person then runs into all the problems we saw in the chapter on epistemology. When someone thinks one molecule "causes" another molecule to move, they then run into Hume's difficult problem of causation. Again, please don't mishear me. I love science. Science is great. But it is not assumption-less. Science rests on the shoulders of philosophical positions and therefore must address the issues related to that field instead of pretending like they don't exist.

If science is like the framing of a house, then philosophy is the concrete slab foundation. You can act like you are just framing a wall without any foundation at all (like many scientists pretend to do), but if you look down you will see that your framing wouldn't be possible at all without a foundation. Since science is not the foundation, it will always lack the perfect objectivity we wish that it had. This is not to disparage science. Science is a tremendous good. Rather, it is to remember that science has a limited job. Its job is to frame the house and not to be the foundation.

Science vs. scientism

Modern science is a tremendous benefit of living in the modern world. As we all know, the reason we didn't get a blister and die from infection when we were children is because science has transformed our daily lives. Scientism, on the other hand, is not the same as science. *Scientism is a set of philosophical and religious beliefs.* Scientism is like an unofficial religion where one assumes that science gets a say in areas in which it is not qualified to play. *Scientism is a worldview.* It is an attempt to act as though science can answer the deepest questions in life, even though those questions don't fall under the category of what science can, de facto, study. Science, when you think about it, is actually a pretty small field of inquiry. It can help us cure those who are sick or advance our smartphones, but it cannot answer our most basic questions such as "What makes something right and wrong?" "Why are we here?" or "What should we believe?"

Each field of study has to "stay in its lane" if it is to be successful. Let's take economics as an example. Economics is an important field of study. If we want to know if the housing market is going to struggle or if our economy is at risk of inflation, then it is an economist whom we should consult. But would you want an economist performing brain surgery on you? Would you want someone with no medical training to cut open your head just because they were good at economics? They might be able to advise you on how to pay for the surgery, but they surely could not perform it. Or, would you want an economist leading a group of soldiers into battle? He could, perhaps, tell you how much the war would cost, but he probably wouldn't know much about small-unit tactics or how to conduct unconventional warfare at night. Conversely, you probably wouldn't want a military general (who would be great at leading soldiers into battle) managing your portfolio in the stock market. He might be personally savvy when it comes to money, but his area of specialty in the military doesn't fully equip him to be a professional economics professor or to advise the White House on future economic trends. The same is true with scientists.

Scientism is where, under the guise of "science," someone tries to implant a *philosophical* notion into the minds of their audience, so that it will be accepted (because everyone wants to be thought of as "scientific"). When you see a well-known scientist giving their opinion on the news regarding issues that are not solely science (such as politics, economics, ethics, religion, public policy, etc.), they are practicing scientism and not science. Their training in chemistry, for example, does not allow them to assess if an action is morally right or wrong. That is the job of the ethicist, not the scientist.

Perhaps the best explanation of scientism can be seen from the COVID-19 pandemic mentioned earlier. Before we dive into this topic, I want to give a clarifier that I'm not giving my position on how COVID should have been handled or my political positions. I understand that the virus, and how we should have responded to it, was very controversial. I'm simply trying to show that the issue was not merely scientific but also political and philosophical.

Science absolutely gets a say in something such as a virus. Science can tell us what the virus does, how it is spread, what treatments do and do not work, and what we can do to avoid getting sick. Science can give us information about a virus. However, *science can't tell us how we should respond to this information.* How we *respond* to it falls under the realms of ethics, public policy, constitutional law, and personal liberty. We might decide that taking a risk for personal liberty is worth the potential danger of the virus. Or we might decide that taking a risk is not something we want to do in light of the danger of the virus. Whether a government decides to mandate lockdowns and masks or decides not to mandate lockdowns and masks are issues related to *constitutional law, public policy, ethics, and a host of other fields of inquiry that go far beyond science.*

The claim that was used on both the political right and the political left was "follow the science." Some scientists said that you should stay home instead of going to the office because you should "follow the science." Other scientists said that you didn't need to stay home because the virus was not deadly to most people, so you should go back to work and "follow the science." The problem was that most people were using the phrase "follow the science" to push some type of political agenda not directly related to how cells and viruses work. That is scientism. All a scientist can do is tell you what COVID does, how it is transmitted, and what the supposed death rate is. *Science cannot tell you how humans should respond to that information.* That would be doing politics and philosophy, not science.

As soon as you tell people what they "ought" to do, you are no longer doing science; you are doing ethics. What humans ought to do falls into the realm of what is good to do. As our old friend David Hume reminds us, science can tell you only what something is, not what it ought to be. We cannot imply an "ought" statement (about what should be the case based upon some higher standard of goodness) from the way something merely "is." *Facts are different than value statements.* Sciences deals with facts, but philosophy deals with value statements. Hume's guillotine, as it is called, helps us see the difference between science and scientism. Science is what is the case in the physical world, but it doesn't get to dictate human action. To say it more clearly, the death rate or the infection rate of COVID implies nothing about what you should do in response to the virus.

The reason I'm continuing with the pandemic example, again, is not to give my views on COVID. I don't care about cultural hot topics. I am simply using the pandemic because *it is the best modern example of scientism with which we are all familiar.* The death rate for COVID-19 (even in the most aggressive estimates) for most people was less than 1%. Some people said that this rate was high and therefore aggressive political action needed to be taken (lockdowns, masks, distancing, vaccine mandates, etc.). Others said that a less than 1% death rate was not very high and therefore aggressive political action did not need to be taken. *Here is what is interesting: notice that both sides are appealing to a fact from science (a death rate of less than 1%), yet for one group of people, that percentage seemed super high, and for another, it seemed super low.*

How on earth is "how people perceive what seems high or low" within the realm of science? Compared to the bubonic plague, COVID was a joke. But compared to the average flu, COVID was serious. Who gets to decide if we compare COVID's severity to the Black Death or influenza? That is a leap away from science into the realm of scientism. It is a veiled form of politics under the guise of science. What many people meant when they said "follow the science" is actually this: "The goal during COVID-19 should be to minimize the deaths and to prevent the spread as much as possible." But that is not a scientific claim; that is a philosophical claim. It is a value claim. It is saying, "The goal during this time should be to minimize death." But why is that the goal? Should avoiding death override every other concern (religious, constitutional, economic, familial, etc.)? As soon as you start answering that question, you realize that you are doing philosophy and politics, not merely science.

That's just one recent example, though scientism occurs in far more places than you would think. When a scientist looks at what animals do in nature and then implies what is ethical about human behavior, that is scientism. When someone assumes that science can answer questions about things that are not material (such as God or numbers), that is scientism. When someone assumes that there are no philosophical presuppositions behind their science, that is scientism.

Science is great. This entire section is not here to disparage science. It is to disparage scientism. It is to help us evaluate science in comparison to scientism. In the same way a guitar doesn't make a very good airplane, we must not deceive ourselves into thinking that something that has a say in only one field somehow stands over other fields just because our culture likes to think that it contains no theories or preset assumptions.

Now that we know what science can and cannot judge, what about entities that science posits that we have never actually experienced? It might blow your mind to know that there are many things that contemporary scientists believe that have never been experienced by any scientists ever.

Actual or theoretical entities?

Within the philosophy of science there is a huge intellectual battle known as the realism versus antirealism debate. Here is the central question: *Do theoretical entities, which we have technically never observed, actually exist in reality, or are they helpful fictions that assist us in practically advancing the use of science in our day-to-day lives?* To say it another way, does science truly explain, or does it merely describe? We like to think that science gives us true knowledge of the world, but it may give us only helpful and practical descriptions.

Is science actually true, or does it merely work really well? That is the central question in this section. Allow me to provide an illustration. Imagine that a doctor created a medicine that cured the common cold. When asked what was in the medicine that actually cured the cold, the doctor said, "The medicine contains bequixens." Now, *bequixens* is a made-up word that I just invented. One cannot see bequixens. They are a theoretical element in the medicine that supposedly cures the cold. The scientist would be praised for finally coming up with a cure for the common cold. But here is the million dollar question: *Do we like the medicine because it works (it cures the cold) or because it actually gives us insight into the truth of the world (by describing bequixens)?* To ask the question more pointedly: Is it relevant at all if bequixens actually exist, if the medicine works regardless of what we know about it? Isn't the entire goal to cure the common cold? Bequixens, in this example, may be real leptons, or they may be a helpful fiction, but "science" has been done either way because the patient was cured. To say "Bequixens cured the cold" and then to ask "What are bequixens?" comes back with the answer "The things that cured the cold." That's a circular definition, especially when we realize that you can't see bequixens—they are just a hypothetical supposition that is used to practically cure the common cold.

What if things such as quarks are just modern-day bequixens?

Consider tectonic plates. Supposedly, there are these massive sheets of rock under the Earth's crust that move and shift, thus accounting for everything from mountain formation to why the continents look the way they do. Here is the kicker: we have never actually directly observed tectonic plates. They are hypothetical entities that help us make sense of the data; the jury is still out on their actual existence. Notice that the issue is not "Does believing in these entities help make sense of the data?" The answer to that question is "Absolutely." The tectonic theory is a smart one. The question is also not "Do tectonic plates most likely exist?" The answer to that question is "Most likely." The question is "Do they really exist, and if we haven't observed them, how did we assume their existence when we can't prove them using the scientific method of observable data?"

Or consider quarks. We have never observed a quark. Is a quark an actually existing thing, or is it something that we postulate (not without evidence, but postulate nevertheless) to help us make sense of other scientific data? This is an issue that bedevils both scientists and philosophers of science. Everything from black holes to magnetic fields falls into the category of entities we think exist that are not strictly observed using the scientific method. Do they actually exist, or do we promote them simply because they "work" when we plug them into our scientific model? After all, as many philosophers have pointed out, the purpose of science is to find something that works—that improves life—not necessarily to give us "knowledge."

Or consider atoms. Most of us grew up hearing that everything is made up of atoms. Not only is it impossible for everything to be made up of atoms (the number two or a vacuum in space, if they do indeed exist, are not made of atoms), we were also told that these tiny spheres called atoms cannot be divided further. But is this information correct? As we mentioned earlier, isn't an atom made up of two half-atoms, and a half-atom made up of two quarter-atoms, and a quarter-atom made up of two eighth-atoms? Can't we at least *conceptually* divide atoms forever? Furthermore, if everything is made up of atoms, why is a desk or a cactus, for example, nothing like an atom? Why is a human nothing like an atom? If I made a tower out of Legos, it would be easy to see that the tower has a lot of properties that a Lego has. But that's not the case with atoms. *Is a desk or cactus really nothing more than tiny spheres and empty space?*

This illustrates the realism verves antirealism debate. Do atoms actually exist, or are they helpful conjectures to help make the other data we find in science "work"? Now, your initial inclination may be to say, "Of course atoms exist, we have seen them." But that is absolutely false. *We have never seen an atom.*

Atoms are theoretical entities that are supposed to be the basic "stuff" out of which everything is made. (Before they were called atoms, they were called corpuscles—atoms are not a new idea). You may think we have seen an atom because you have seen a black-and-white video of someone "cutting" an atom and a bunch of liquidy goo spilling out everywhere. But (1) that would mean that atoms are not the building blocks of life but whatever is actually in them, and (2) that was not an atom that was cut. That was a tiny piece of material. An actual atom, *by definition*, is something that cannot be further divided. (The Greek word, *atomos*, literally means "uncuttable.") Or you may think that we divided atoms by making the atomic bomb. But this commits the logical fallacy of "begging the question"—where one assumes the conclusion in the argument's premise. The realist will say that there are actual atoms and we divided them to create an explosion. But the antirealist will say that atoms are just a helpful fiction for modeling how we understand the nuclear reaction going on in the bomb; it doesn't actually show that these atoms exist. All it shows is that we can make really big explosions. We assume the "atoms" are doing the exploding, but we don't see the atoms; we see only the explosion.

Science is notorious for given names to entities that may not actually exist. Perhaps the most famous one is the name *gravity*. Philosophers (especially our atheist friend, Hume) mocked scientists after Newton for assuming that "gravity" is what pulls things to the ground. Now, before we go any further, I need to clarify something that almost every beginning student of philosophy misunderstands. By making fun of the concept of gravity, Hume (and others) are not saying that things don't fall down. They are not saying that if you throw a ball up in the air, it will just stay there. Hume, in fact, did not fly off the ground when he opposed the idea of gravity. They are not denying that things fall to the earth or that large objects attract smaller ones. They all agree with that. They are not denying the phenomenon that we today call gravity. *The reaon they are poking fun of scientists is for thinking that just because you gave some observed phenomena a name, "gravity," you thereby know what it actually is.* Giving something a name is not the same as actually knowing it.

To further elaborate on this point, consider the following example. If I throw a ball up into the air and it falls back down, I may ask, "What caused the ball to fall to the ground?" You will probably say, "Gravity." I then ask, "What is this mysterious 'gravity' of which you speak?," to which you will reply, "It is the thing that caused it to fall to the ground." *Do you see that you just argued in a logical circle?* I asked what made the ball fall to the ground and you said, "Gravity." But when I then asked what gravity was, you simply said, "The thing that caused it to fall to the ground." You didn't actually explain *why* the ball fell to the ground. You just called the phenomena we observed (the ball falling to the ground) gravity. When I then asked what gravity was, you had no definition other than the very thing we are trying to define. When I ask what it is that makes a ball fall to the ground and you say, "Gravity," you can't then define gravity by saying it is what makes a ball fall to the ground. I already know the ball falls to the ground. I'm asking what actually makes it do that. I'm not asking what name you give to the action of a ball falling to the ground.

Imagine that I said there was this mythical, spiritual force called oogabooga. I tell you that oogabooga causes things to move at a distance and oogabooga is what makes an apple fall to the Earth. You think to yourself, "I see that apples fall to the earth, but I'm not sure this force that we cannot see called 'oogabooga' is doing it." Now you understand Hume's critique of gravity. Gravity is like oogabooga. Hume is not critiquing the fact that things fall down; he doesn't think things fall up. *Rather, he is showing a deficiency in science when a scientist merely gives a new name to an observed phenomenon and we thereby think that entity really exists.*

Consider, for example, when a deodorant company advertises that their deodorant now contains "odor-fighting technology." What on earth is odor-fighting technology? The simple answer is that odor-fighting technology is merely the deodorant itself. Deodorant, by its very odor-fighting nature, is made to resist body odor. All they have done is merely make the deodorant more "deodorant-y." But they are using a brand new phrase (i.e., odor-fighting technology) to make you think they have done something that no other brand of deodorant has ever done. They are using a particular phrase that sounds scientific ("technology"), though it is merely another label for whatever is in deodorant that resists odor. To say a "deodorant fights odor" and to say a "deodorant has odor-fighting technology" mean the same thing. Hume would point out that "things fall to the ground" and "gravity causes things to fall to the ground" actually mean the same thing.

Or consider sudden infant death syndrome (SIDS). This is a medical term used for the heartbreaking occurrence of a child passing away when we don't know the actual cause of death. It is a label that we give to a child's death so that we can feel scientific. After all, we aren't humble enough to say that we simply don't know why the baby died. SIDS is not an actual cause of death. It is not something that someone can catch from another or something we can put in a test tube. Rather, it is a label we give to something when we don't really know what stands behind it.

None of these examples makes the question about real versus theoretical entities any easier. We are still inclined to believe that gravity is more than just a name attached to the fact that things fall down. And we are still inclined to believe that there are little atoms that compose larger things. But why do we think that if we haven't really observed them? Do the theories in science work because they are close to reality, or are they merely pragmatic? At the end of the day there are good cases that can be made either way, but since they are logically contradictory, they can't both be right. Perhaps science has more philosophy hiding under the surface than most people like to admit.

In 1942 Albert Camus wrote a famous philosophical article (which would end up winning him the Nobel Prize in Literature) called "The Myth of Sisyphus." In this brilliant article, Camus shows how absurd life is in light of our desire to understand everything rationally and how nonrational life seems to be. He has a fascinating comment early in the work about how science seems to be rational until it makes a leap into theoretical entities. We think we will finally understand the world until we push the scientist further. He says:

> *And here are trees and I know their gnarled surface, water and I feel its taste. These scents of grass and stars at night, certain evenings when the heart relaxes—how shall I negate this world whose power and strength I feel? Yet all the knowledge on earth will give me nothing to assure me that this world is mine. You describe it to me and you teach me to classify it. You enumerate its laws and in my thirst for knowledge I admit that they are true. You take apart its mechanism and my hope increases. At the final state you teach me that this wonderous and multicolored universe can be reduced to the atom and that the atom itself can be reduced to the electron. All this is good and I wait for you to continue. But you tell me of*

an invisible planetary system in which electrons gravitate around a nucleus. You explain this world to me with an image. I realize then that you have been reduced to poetry. . . . So that science, that was to teach me everything ends up in a hypothesis.[9]

Teleology

Teleology is the study of end or purpose (the Greek word, *telos*, means "end," "purpose," or "goal"). In science, we run into the concept of teleology when we try to discuss why something does what it does. Notice that when a scientist says that a frog has evolved "in order to stay alive" or "to give itself a reproductive advantage" or "to better defend against predators," they are using the concept of *purpose*. They are doing much more than science; they are doing teleology. They are not saying that a frog merely has changed. They are saying something much more. *They are saying that there is an intelligent reason for why the frog changed; they are saying there is a reason or a purpose behind it.*

Things don't just randomly happen, according to most biologists (though this idea is disputed by scientists who promote certain forms of quantum mechanics). Rather, there is a purpose or goal for what happens. We say this all the time when discussing science (especially biology). The reason the hair on your eyebrows grows up and to the side is to keep sweat out of your eyes. That's a purpose. The reason a female deer mates with a strong buck is because it will allow her offspring to have a higher chance of being strong and healthy. That's a purpose. The reason plants develop thorns is to protect themselves from animals that may try to eat them. That's a purpose. And, with the thorn example, this (intelligent) purpose happens even though plants don't have cognitive capacities like animals or humans.

So far, so good. So what's the big deal with teleology? All the above statements make sense to us, so why is this even something we are discussing? Here is where it becomes tricky: *teleology presupposes something more than just matter; it presupposes some mind.* Reread that last sentence again. Purposes and goals presuppose some intelligence beyond random matter. To say that something has a goal or a purpose makes absolutely no sense if everything is just random particles moving around in space. You may think that humans are smart and that we use our minds to make decisions, plan goals, and work toward purposes. That's true. How then did whatever the smallest particles in the universe are come together to form thinking things if they themselves were unthinking? How did beings who can think come together from unthinking matter? How can you have goals or purposes (for anything in nature) without some mind or intelligence (even before humans)?

We want to say the plant grows thorns *in order to ward off predators,* but true science won't allow us to say that. It allows us only to say that the plant has thorns. It may be a convenient truth that thorns do indeed ward off hungry animals. But that can be only an inference we draw philosophically; we cannot say they developed thorns for that *purpose* without presupposing some directing mind. But this seems to put science in conflict with religion. On the one hand, the religious person believes teleology is evidence for their position—there must be a Mind (capital *M*) such as God who has given purpose to all that is. The nonreligious person, in contrast, would not agree, but they are left doing the difficult work of describing how there can be purposes in nature, especially before things have evolved enough for there to be true "thinking" without some larger Mind.

Many philosophers have critiqued science for just this issue. *Science often says more than what is directly experienced.* Science often goes beyond the bounds of the scientific method because it wants to play in the realm of teleology. But it cannot do that. Science can say, "Plants have thorns and animals do not eat those plants," but it cannot say, "Plants developed thorns *in order to* ward off predators." Science can say, "The hair on one's eyebrows grows up and to the side; when one sweats, the sweat goes around the eyes," but it cannot say, "The hair on our eyebrows grows up and to the side *in order to* keep sweat out of our eyes." Science can say, "Fish swim in schools, thus decreasing their risk of being eaten," but it cannot say, "Fish swim in schools *in order to* avoid being eaten." Do you see the difference in these examples between what science can and can't say? Science must simply describe what is (what is physical). When it tries to go beyond that, it has to bring in notions of intelligence and purpose (which are not physical). Do you see how even something that we think of as objective and sense-based actually rests on philosophical assumptions?

So, this brings up the million-dollar question: If philosophy has a say in science and some science is bogus, how do we know true science from pseudoscience? What litmus test can we use to distinguish true science (like particle physics) from false science (such as eugenics)? The answer is in a term called falsification.

Falsification

Imagine a man who went into his doctor's office claiming to have the limbs of his body moved, not by electrical impulses in his nervous system but by fairies or sprites who flew around pushing his arms. The doctor, in addition to probably requesting a full psychological evaluation, would likely seek to explain to the man that what moved his limbs were his muscles, which were, in turn, directed by electric and chemical impulses from the brain. But what if the man persisted? What if he continued to swear that it was actually tiny little Tinkerbells that were moving his limbs? The doctor, in this case, would be at an impasse. No evidence that you can show the patient will change his mind. He has moved beyond the realm of reason and into the realm of confirmation bias.

This is why the philosopher, Karl Popper, is so important to the philosophy of science. What Popper proposed was the idea that for an idea to really be within the realm of science (or what intelligent people should even consider science), it had to be falsifiable. *There had to be a way of proving a scientific theory wrong.* This didn't mean that a particular scientific theory was actually wrong; it just meant that there had to be grounds given that could prove it wrong *if these grounds were met.* It had to have the possibility of being wrong. If a position was presented but did not have any criteria whereby it could be disproved, then it was not really science.

Proving a theory a lot of times is not what makes something scientifically valid. After all, many people were bled when they had fevers and their fevers eventually went away. This led doctors (three hundred years ago) to believe that they had a lot of proof for the idea that bleeding people with fevers was a good, scientific approach. *Proving a theory doesn't necessarily mean it's true. Rather, there has to be a way to disprove it.*

There must be a way to disprove a theory if it is really "science." If a theory doesn't have grounds that would make it untrue (if they could be discovered), then the person who holds that theory is arguing in a circle. They would be stating that their position was right, and then when someone asked them what would make them change their mind, they are essentially saying, "Nothing." For Popper, you can't say "nothing." *If you are doing science, you have to give the grounds that would change your mind if counterevidence could be demonstrated.* What Popper is trying to do is to distinguish what makes something science from what makes another thing pseudoscience. Astrology and alchemy claim to be sciences, but most would agree they are pseudosciences. But how do we know? We need a demarcation principle that distinguishes real versus fake claims of sciences. Popper provides us with the answer: *there must be clear criteria that would prove it to be wrong.*

Imagine someone said that there was a magical, invisible unicorn in the room, but you couldn't feel, smell, taste, touch, hear, or see the unicorn. How would you disprove their claim? They could try to "prove" that the invisible unicorn was really there, and because they kept "proving" it (at least to themselves), then their claim would have to be taken as science. It's pretty difficult to prove that a unicorn that you can't perceive doesn't exist. Popper protects us from absurd claims like this. Popper lets us know that there has to be a way to falsify (show to be false) their claim, for it to be a real claim in science. If there is no way of showing that the invisible unicorn doesn't really exist, then we are not bound to take the person's ridiculous claim as credible.

Popper uses the twin examples of Freud's psychoanalysis and Marx's Marxism as examples of pseudoscience because there is no scientific way to disprove them if they happened to be false.[10] For example, if someone is following Freud's view that we are driven by the subconscious, there is no way to disprove that, because by nature we can only really know consciousness. The Freudian could say that you cheated on your wife *because you suppressed your sexuality* or (conversely) that you stayed faithful to your spouse *because you suppressed your sexuality.* The same position (psychoanalysis) could be used to argue either case. This is psudoscience to thinkers like Popper. Or consider Marxism. There is no way to disprove Marxism. If the Marxist project ever doesn't work, they will just claim that it "wasn't real Marxism." Marxism is assumed to be true, and no matter how many millions die in the gulags, the true Marxist won't admit that the theory has been falsified.

For many scientists before Popper, there was too much confirmation bias. A scientist would prove a theory "right" and then just keep trying to do things that would continue to leave the theory unchallenged. If, for example, you think that smoking doesn't cause lung cancer and you keep doing experiments that prove that it doesn't cause lung cancer, then you're not really doing science. You've just kept confirming what you already assumed. Rather, you must try to prove that smoking does cause cancer. Only after you have tried to falsify your original position can you be said to have done science.

Popper's falsification principle has been used by many people to critique religious claims. For example, it has been used against Christians, Muslims, and Jews to say that the idea of creationism (or creation science) is not a real claim to objective knowledge (or not a real science) *because there is no way to disprove it.* What evidence could be given to prove the theist's account of the universe incorrect (since they begin with the assumption that God made everything, and we can't go back to see what happened)?

Conversely (and controversially), the falsification principle has been used to say the claims of transgenderism are not scientific. *This is because it requires those who identify as transgender to give an objective criterion for what could prove them wrong if it could be presented.* For example, if someone was born biologically male but now identifies as female, the student of Popper would ask, "What evidence could be given that would disprove your claim of now being female and show it to be false?" The person asking this question is wanting to know what could convince a trans person that their preferred identity was incorrect. Since the transgender community does not have a specific criterion of gender authentication, the future of the falsification principle as it relates to this contemporary hot-button issue is yet to be determined. How should one think of a scientific issue (such as biological sex) when it relates to issues not directly related to science (such as how one identifies internally)?

To be clear, many philosophers believe that Popper's theory is necessary but not sufficient—meaning, for something to be science, there must be a demarcation principle to disprove false theories. But is that enough? Is there anything else needed to prove something scientific than the mere fact that there is a way to disprove it? What about theories that seem to be scientific that can't be disproved (such as our knowledge of the origins of the universe)? Neither the theist nor the materialist can go back in time to see what happened. So, to what level is cosmology subject to this principle?

Does science get closer to reality over time?

We often think that science gets us closer and closer to reality as time goes on. If we are trying to get from *a* to *z*, we like to think that people in the ancient world started at *a*. By the time we get to the Enlightenment, we are at the letter *g*. By the time we get to Einstein we are at the letter *m*, and one day, we will finally make it to the letter *z*. We like to think that science follows a linear pattern. We like to think that science doesn't really have alternative theories or alternative methods. We like to think that we are getting closer and closer to knowing everything that can be known. This assumption is that science progresses over time; we start with a system, and most of scientific history just fills in the gaps of that system.

These assumptions, however, may be incorrect. What if science doesn't follow a linear pattern but rather is altered with significantly new paradigms that replace earlier theories?[11] We like to think that science "progresses"— and that may be true if by progresses we mean "makes life more enjoyable." But if by progresses we mean "comes to truer knowledge of ultimate existence by building on previous theories without deviation," then our assumptions may be a bit naïve.

For most of Western history, following Aristotle, it was believed that the Earth was the center of the solar system. When it was discovered that heliocentrism was correct (that the sun was actually at the center of our solar system), then the previous system was replaced by a new system. *In this example, it is not the case that science merely built more knowledge upon the old system (geocentrism). Rather, a completely new paradigm replaced an older one.* This is a pretty radical thought if you allow yourself to concentrate on it. Scientific "breakthroughs" are often nothing less than a complete replacement of a previous system. In this sense, science doesn't progress. Rather, a new theory simply replaces an older theory. Einstein replaces Newton in a big way; he doesn't just build off of Newton. Heliocentrism replaces geocentrism in a big way; it doesn't just build off of geocentrism.

We now know that humans are made from the combination of sperm and egg. The mother contributes half, and the father contributes half. But this hasn't always been what scientists thought regarding human conception. A common view in the ancient Near East, for example, was that both men and women produced a type of seed. The male produced sperm, and the woman's vaginal wetness was considered her "seed." Whoever produced more seed would determine if the baby was male or female. During the Middle Ages, many believed that the man produced the full baby in his sperm. He produced a *homunculus* or a tiny human. The woman, condescendingly, was simply seen as an incubator or oven for the tiny human to grow into a baby. This is why King Henry the VIII got so mad at his wives (whom he kept beheading). In his mind, if they would just be better incubators, then he could have a son to reign on his throne instead of daughters (which, due to Aristotle, were seen as incomplete males). "Why," you may ask, "does a child sometimes look like its mother if she is just an incubator and the full human comes from the male sperm?" Well, for the same reason that if you leave a popsicle in the freezer too long, it begins to taste like "freezer," so they thought that a baby looks like its mother because she was the oven in which the baby resided for so long.

Why are we going over a quick history of how scientists thought that humans were conceived (other than seeing that some of their views were a bit sexist)? The answer is that science, in these examples, didn't just build off of previous theories. In many cases, science doesn't grow. One theory is dominant and is then replaced, wholesale, with a new theory.

The hope that we are "progressing" in our knowledge might be nothing more than hope after all. What scientific theories do we now hold that will be laughable from the perspective of future generations? If it is true that our entire view of the solar system was wrong back then, what other systems that are "true" today will be replaced with better paradigms in the future?

After all, you may be inclined to say that what people did back then wasn't really science. But couldn't future generations say that about us? Will scientists one thousand years from now view us the way we view the scientists of the Middle Ages?

Conclusion

Perhaps no other field of modern inquiry has impacted humanity more over the last hundred years than science and technology. We live longer, more comfortable lives because brilliant men and women have created a myriad of medical and technological innovations. But does this mean that science merely works or that it gives us actual knowledge? What about theoretical entities? What do we do when scientists disagree?

Science is great; but it is not logic. It is not purely objective, and it is limited to probabilities about the observable world. It can tell us how to make medicine, how to advance a smartphone, and how to increase wheat crops through genetic modifications. But it can't answer some of the deepest questions of our existence.

One of the things science cannot do is tell us what is right or wrong. We may see a lion attack a gazelle in nature, but we don't see whether this is "good" or "bad" (what color or shape, after all, is goodness)? In fact, the most educated and scientifically advanced nation in 1942 was Nazi Germany. Their learning, regretfully, didn't help them be more moral. To know right and wrong, we must study ethics. It is this topic to which we will turn in our next chapter.

Ethics

ETHICS IS THE STUDY of morality and what makes something good or right. Ethics is unique in the examination of philosophy, but not because we don't follow the same logical methods or approaches in studying this topic as we do in the other topics. Rather, what makes ethics unique is that *it affects us in a way that is much more personal.*

When one studies metaphysics, per se, the conclusions are interesting. Whatever position we adopt changes how we view the world. When one studies the philosophy of science, the conclusions are interesting. Whatever position we adopt changes how we approach methodological issues related to things such as medicine. But when one studies ethics, in contrast, we step into an area that is not merely interesting *but one that affects the very core of the actions and decisions we make every day.* Whereas topics such as metaphysics deal with what *is*, ethics deals with value statements.

The debate between rationalism and empiricism is interesting. But debates about whether or not abortion should be legal, to what degree we should care for the planet, or whether or not the CIA can use painful interrogation methods to extract information from captured terrorists are questions that passionately impact us. When we are dealing with ethics, there is something very visceral and emotional about the questions we encounter. We are no longer wondering whether or not some dead philosopher had a correct ancient proof for some obscure position. Rather, we are trying to figure out how to live our lives and how to interact with the people around us. We may accept that we might be poorer, less educated, shorter, or less attractive than other people; those are inequalities with which we can live. But we become quite upset when someone accuses us of being immoral.

Why is that? Why do we naturally accept inequalities of education or physical strength, for example, but are so uncomfortable with moral inequalities? If someone says "You are not as strong as that bodybuilder," we may not like that statement, but it doesn't really affect us. But if someone says "You are immoral compared to that person," we become agitated. There is something about us that doesn't want to be thought of as immoral. We like to think we are "good people" even if we are not.

Not only does ethics contain important questions, it also contains questions that are difficult to answer. Is morality objective for all cultures, or is it culturally defined? Are certain actions always wrong, or do they change depending upon the circumstances? Is morality objective or subjective? Should ethics be based on what is best for you or what is best for others, even if it is not what is best for you? Should we consider the outcome of our actions (when pondering whether or not an action is moral), or should we just look at the morality of the action itself, regardless of the consequences?

These are the higher-level questions—the meta-questions, if you will—within the field of ethics. But there are issues that hit far closer to home that pertain to the practical implementation of ethics. Consider these questions: What counts as "marriage," and who gets to decide? Do humans have an obligation to take care of the environment, and to what extent? Should people be allowed to own guns to protect their (innocent) lives, or does that put the (innocent) lives of others at risk? Which sexual acts are immoral, if any, and what counts as consent? What is racism, and is it intrinsic for all people within a majority culture, or is it an intentional mindset of ethnic hatred? Is it always wrong to lie, and if not, what criteria must be met before a lie is not immoral? Is tolerance a virtue, and should there then be tolerance towards others who are not tolerant? Can immoral actions be committed by groups or only individuals in that group (since a group is made up only of singular individuals anyway)? Can you kill an animal for sport, even if you don't eat the meat? You see . . . ethics isn't just "head in the clouds" thinking. If affects our politics, families, safety, interactions, and just about every part of our daily lives.

Throughout this chapter we will be looking at what makes something right or wrong and why.

Two incomplete systems

One way to answer the question about what makes something right or wrong is to say "nothing"—nothing makes something right or wrong. It is to say that good and bad are not real categories. There are some philosophers who think that ethics, as a concept, isn't really an objective thing at all. To these philosophers, we may prefer not to be raped or murdered or assaulted, but we cannot say that it is objectively "wrong." Things just happen, and there is no actual morality to which humans should strive. If we are simply evolved apes and the universe is just a bunch of matter bumping around in the cosmos, then morality is a made-up category. We cannot say that "it is wrong to assault a child," because there is no ultimately higher standard of right or wrong to which we can attach that sentence. We can say that our society frowns on assaulting children or that we personally find it abhorrent, but (if one holds this worldview) they cannot say that it is universally and objectively wrong. We cannot say that the Holocaust was objectively bad but merely that many people find it offensive and that it should be avoided if it doesn't fit in with the prevailing cultural opinions. To be clear, some of the philosophers who hold this position believe that there are ethical systems. They just don't believe there is a meta-ethic to which these systems correspond. They believe there are systems of ethics but that those systems are not grounded in a larger, objective ethic.

This is the view of both subjectivism and moral relativism. Technically, these are distinct—*subjectivism* is the view that ethics is merely one's opinion, and *relativism* is the idea that contradictory ethical opinions can both be true at the same time—but I will use the term *relativism* to refer to either view. Moral relativism comes in many different flavors. Some don't believe in morality at all. They would hold that cultures have competing values, but none of them are right in reality, because morality is not objective. Others believe that differing truth claims can be true of one culture but not true of another. For one culture, cannibalism may be thought to be good, and therefore it is good *for them*. But another culture may think that cannibalism is bad, and so it is bad *for them*. But either way, both groups do not believe in a higher standard of goodness that allows them to objectively understand certain moral axioms as binding upon humanity.

The reason I say that this answer to the question "What makes something right or wrong?" is incomplete is that it both (1) seems contradictory and (2) strikes us as completely detached from reality. First of all, if one culture thinks infanticide is good and another thinks it's bad, they can't both be right. We could say that infanticide is *considered* good for one and *considered* good for another, but that is not the question about which most of us care. We want to know if infanticide is good or bad, period. We want to know if infanticide is good or bad in reality, for all humans, regardless of specific cultures. If everything is culturally determined, these two competing truth claims will break against the rock of the law of noncontradiction.

Second, most of us are not willing to go in this direction because of its profound implications. Do you really believe that a white supremacist can go around shouting the N-word and they are not wrong in so doing? Even if it is legal, is it good? Do you really believe that the Holocaust was just an event that happened but that the Nazis were not somehow actually *wrong* in murdering six million Jewish people? Do you really think that a person who sexually assaults a baby is doing something that could be good as long as it is considered good *to them* or to their culture? Does a tribal chief have a right to rape a woman just because his tribe believes that the king can do whatever he wants? When a deranged teenager shoots up a school or drowns baby animals in his bathtub just for fun, are these events simply happening (without a moral quality), or is there some moral content that goes along with the actions?

Most of us are not willing to say that the Holocaust merely happened. Rather, we say that it was *wrong*. Most of us are not willing to say that someone who is a pedophile is merely committing an act with an underaged child but that they are *wrong* in doing so. In fact, our entire justice system is based on the fact that we believe people should be punished by the state for their evil actions. And the reason we think they should be punished is because they did something objectively evil. Even the thief thinks that it is wrong when someone steals from him. Even pirates have a "pirate code" by which they conduct their villainy. Even an adulterer may get mad when his wife cheats on him. Even a cartel boss gets upset if another cartel leader lies to him. At the end of the day, as much as we like to pretend that morality is completely relative, arbitrary, or culturally conditioned, we bump up against issues that strike at the heart of justice itself. When this happens, we are less likely to say "That's just your view" and more likely to say "That's wrong."

The second view that is incomplete is what is called divine command theory. This is the idea that what makes something right or wrong is that God (or the gods, in polytheistic religions) have said that some act is right or wrong. Anytime I teach about ethics and ask what makes something right or wrong, the first answer that many people shout out is that it does or does not conform to the Bible (or some other book of revealed religion). Let me say from the outset that this is actually not a terrible answer. *After all, if God does indeed exist, then he would be the absolute standard of goodness and his commands would literally be what makes something right or wrong.* This is not a wrong answer when one really thinks about it. It is a consistent and well-attested view of morality stretching back millennia. The reason I say it is incomplete, in addition to the fact that someone who does not believe in God will instantly dismiss it, is because *it only pushes the morality question back further instead of answering it*—meaning, it doesn't deal with the ultimate question we are asking. Allow me to explain with four reasons on why divine command theory is incomplete:

First, if the reason murder is wrong is because God has commanded that we should not murder, that simply leads to the further question of "Why does God think we should not murder?" This is what is known as the Euthyphro dilemma. *Is something good simply because God says it is good, or is the very reason God says it is good is because he sees that it is already good?* To say it another way, does God command us not to murder because God's intellect sees that murder is inherently evil for humans to whom he has ascribed value (called *intellectualism*), or is the only reason that murder is evil is because God's will has decided that it would be evil (called *voluntarism*). Is God's command the only thing that makes an act evil? To put even a finer point on it, if God had commanded us to sexually assault each other, would that act cease to be evil and actually be good for the sole reason that God, the source of all good, commanded us to do so? There is not an easy answer to this question, and many philosophers disagree.

If you say that God declares something good because it is already good, that makes it sound as if there is some form or standard above God called goodness to which God must conform. This seems to severely limit God's power and freedom to have created the world any way he wanted and to have commanded anything he wanted. But if you say that the only reason that a command is good (or that a prohibition is bad) is because God simply decided it should be so, it seems to make God a bit arbitrary. If God had indeed commanded us to harm as many people as we could, we would probably not worship that version of God (even though he is God!) because it feels as though God would be evil—he would not be meeting some standard of morality. But how could there be a standard of morality above God? If he is all-powerful and all-good, then his commands would be the final arbiter on all things. Just because we may not know why God commands something does not mean that he doesn't have a reason. What seems "arbitrary" to us may not be arbitrary to him. Either way, we want to know if some things are inherently good, even to God.

Second, in divine command theory, when trying to understand God's commands, how are we supposed to know what they are? We don't just have a Tanach, we have an *interpreted* Tanach. We don't just have a Koran, we have an *interpreted* Koran. We don't just have a Bible, we have an *interpreted* Bible. We don't just have the Vedas, we have the *interpreted* Vedas. Though many religious people believe that what makes something right or wrong is that God has commanded it, we still run into the issue of figuring out exactly what God has commanded.

When one reads the Bible, for example, they are not merely reading it but *interpreting* it. As soon as you are doing interpretation you are doing a subset of philosophy called *hermeneutics* (which is the science and study of interpretation). Though Christians attempt to follow the Bible, they break off into different denominations because they don't agree on exactly what God has commanded and why. When Sunni or Shia Muslims disagree on how to interpret the Koran, they are running into the same issue. Many people want to follow God's commands, but sometimes knowing exactly what God's commands are becomes tricky. It's difficult to have a divine book to follow without also having a divine hermeneutics textbook that tells you how to interpret it.

Third, when appealing to the commands of a God, one isn't just following a set of divine rules. *Rather, the person must first pick which religious system they want to follow.* It is not the case that one can just follow what God has said. *First, one must decide which religious system their God belongs to—and this is an ethical decision.* Before one can follow God's commands, they must ask, "Should I follow the commands of Allah in Islam or of Ganesh in Hinduism?" Or they may ask, "Should I submit to God's commands as interpreted by the Catholic church or the Lutheran church?" Or they may ask, "Should I submit to God's commands in Judaism or to wise principles in Shintoism?" Or they may ask, "Should I interpret the Bible literally or figuratively?" *In this sense a person is deciding which divine commands to submit to before even adopting divine command theory.* One first makes a leap toward a religion and, only after, decides to submit to the deity of that religion. Even when one wants to follow God's commands, they are not excused from the moral decision of which God (or gods) they think exist and how those gods are to be understood.

To say it another way, as soon as one decides that they want to follow God's commands in the Bible, that decision itself was not something they read in the Bible. They may read it in the Bible later, but that initial step was a presupposition that they didn't get from the Bible. They didn't start with God's commands; they started with their decision. What causes that first step where one decides which religious book they want to begin reading?

Fourth, and most importantly, you will still have to develop an ethical method that you adopt, even if you believe that what makes something right or wrong is that God (or the gods) have commanded it. This is why I said divine command theory could be defended, but it is still an incomplete system. For example, the Bible commands people not to murder. (It does not command that they may not righteously kill, such as in self-defense or war, but that they may not unrighteously kill, which is the definition of murder.) So far, so good. But what counts as murder as new events not directly addressed in the Bible arise? Is in vitro fertilization murder because several fertilized eggs will perish in the process? If several embryos are created (and if life starts at conception for the Christian), then would it not be murder if all those embryos were not implanted into the mother but rather disposed of or left in a freezer? You see, though we have a command not to murder, we are going to have to do philosophy to figure out how to apply it when new situations (not addressed in a divine book) arise.

Or consider this, though the Bible does not forbid drinking, it does forbid getting drunk. How should we apply this command to something that the Bible doesn't address directly, such as the use of marijuana in places where it is legal? Is the state of being "high" the same as being "drunk"? Whereas alcohol has a long runway before one is drunk, weed has a much shorter runway before one is high. Does this mean that one could smoke marijuana in moderation? How do we apply this biblical command to the issue of legalized marijuana? Or consider the fact that the Bible commands us not to lie. That sounds simple enough. But what if we are hiding Jews in our basement in 1943 in Germany and the SS asks if we are hiding any Jews? Can we lie then? Is it an unethical to lie in this unique situation? Should we be like the biblical character Rahab who lied to protect God's Hebrew spies in the Old Testament? What if we are a spy or an undercover police officer, are we always bound to tell bad guys who we are? We may think that commands that forbid lying or stealing are pretty simple, but we instantly have to start doing philosophy if we are lying to protect someone's life or stealing food to feed our family when we are starving. Or, what if there is a moral issue that the Bible doesn't seem to address at all, at least directly and explicitly, such as who to vote for in a democracy when you have candidates who both hold (at least some) important issues not addressed in Scripture?

The problem with both the ethical relativist and the divine command theorist is not that they are wrong (logically, either could be correct). The problem with each adherent is that they are a bit lazy; *they don't do the hard work of consistently dealing with all the objections that plague their respective systems.* If there is no objective morality or if morality is dictated by God, there is still a lot of difficult philosophical work to be done before we have a fully formed system of ethics.

Relativism may be correct, but it will still need a persuasive way to deal with the important issues that arise throughout our lives. Divine command theory may be correct, but it will probably have to be combined with one of the other ethical systems for it to be complete (such as utilitarianism, deontology, etc.). In this sense one might be not just a Jew, Muslim, or Christian but a Jewish *virtue ethicist*, or a Muslim *utilitarian*, or a Christian *deontologist*, for example. Regardless of religion, one must still adopt an ethical grid to which they can attach their divine commands.

In what follows we will look at four different ethical scenarios and try to decide how we would respond in each situation. We will accomplish this by looking at several larger ethical systems and seeing how a proponent of each would address each of the four scenarios.

Four test cases

Scenario 1: You are a German citizen during WWII, and you are hiding Jews in your basement. A Nazi officer knocks on your door and asks you if you are hiding any Jews (or what he calls "enemies of the state"). Is it unethical to lie to protect the lives of the Jews? Notice that the question is not "What would you do in this situation?" Most of us would lie to protect the Jewish people. The question is "*Have you done something wrong or unethical by lying,* even if you did the right thing by not handing over the Jews?"

Scenario 2: You are a Navy SEAL sent in to kill a known terrorist leader. As you approach the terrorist's village, an innocent shepherd boy sees your team. If you don't kill the boy, he will tell the terrorist leader about your team (which will cause the terrorist to get away, cause your team to be in danger, and will lead to the deaths of many more people whom the terrorist will kill). Do you kill the innocent child to prevent more total deaths from happening? This is the exact plot of the book and movie *Lone Survivor,*[12] and it presents an interesting ethical question.

Scenario 3: You have been captured by a sadistic killer who has fifty people chained up in a compound far away from the general population. The killer has a young woman kneel down before you and says, "If you murder this woman with your bare hands, then I will let you and all fifty people go free, but if you are unwilling to kill her, then I will kill you and all fifty people." For the purpose of this example the killer is actually telling the truth—he will truly let the others go free if you murder the woman—and you also can't do anything other than decide to kill her or not. (You can't try to kill the killer or use your James Bond skills to get away.) What do you do?

Scenario 4: You are the president of the US toward the end of WWII. Do you decide to drop the atomic bombs on Japan? The Japanese have told you that they will never surrender. If you don't drop the nuclear bombs, then many more American troops will be killed, a mainland invasion of Japan must commence, and the fighting could continue for years. If you do drop the bombs, you know that you will be vaporizing many people who, at least at the present time, are not yet soldiers (but still civilians). Do you drop the warheads? Again, for this scenario, these are your only two options.

Ethical systems

With these four scenarios in mind, we will now turn to looking at several larger ethical systems. We will observe what each system says about ethics generally and how each system would answer the four scenarios above. Though there are many different subsets and combinations of ethical systems in addition to relativism and divine command theory, there are three primary paradigms to which almost all ethical decisions adhere. These are the systems of deontology, utilitarianism, and virtue ethics.

Before we list these systems, allow me to use an overly simple and crude summary (because it makes ethics easier to learn, and I love making philosophy accessible to people). At the end of the day most people's ethical systems really boil down to one of two general methods. (1) Some people think that an action is right or wrong based upon the outcome of that action, and (2) others think that an action is right or wrong based on the action itself, regardless of the consequences. Most of our ethical thinking comes down to choosing one of these two approaches. If we think of scenario 3 above (the one where you are told that you have to murder the woman to save the lives of fifty strangers) some people instantly want to say that you should kill the woman because it will practically save more lives (i.e., an action is right or wrong depending upon the consequences of the action instead of the action itself). Others will say that killing the woman is murder, and murder is wrong because unrighteous killing is inherently, logically, and universally wrong for all people (i.e., an action is right or wrong in and of itself, regardless of the consequences). Our first two systems directly address this issue though they come to radically different conclusions.

Deontology

Let's begin with deontology. This is a fancy word for a system of ethics that focuses on one's rational and ethical duty (the Greek word, *deon*, simply means "duty"). The proponent of this system believes that the consequences for one's actions are not the deciding factor for what counts as right and wrong. Rather, the *action itself* is what determines morality. We could summarize deontological ethics this way: *an act is right or wrong depending upon logical, obligatory, universal rules to which all people are bound by duty.*

Notice a few things about this explanation. First, it doesn't care about the consequences. This system does not believe that consequences are what make an action right or wrong. Second, notice that it is bound to rationality. Unlike an ethical system based on emotion or subjectivity, it is a system that tries to be logically consistent and intellectually accessible to all people. This is also something that sets it apart from divine command theory. Divine commands are known only by adherents of a religion or only through access to sacred texts. But this form of ethics is available to all people who are willing to think critically. No special revelation is required. Additionally, notice that the rules are universal. It's not just that people in Russia shouldn't lie but people in Botswana can lie; all people shouldn't lie. Also notice that it is doing one's duty that makes an action right or wrong—doing what one "ought" to do is central to this system.

This is the ethical system that belongs to Immanuel Kant. Other people had held that ethics are universal for all people and that an action is right or wrong in and of itself before Kant. What Kant did, however, was to ground this idea in *reason* by establishing a coherent system of ethics based on duty. Kant's grid through which he sifts ethical decisions is what is known as his famous "categorical imperative." There is not just one version of the categorical imperative (Kant changes it slightly throughout his works), but a good summary would be:

> *Act so that the maxim may be capable of becoming a universal law for all rational beings.*[13]

This sounds technical, but essentially the idea is that when thinking through an ethical decision, we should turn that decision into a general rule for all people and see if that results in a logical contradiction or not.

For example, let's say I'm thinking about telling a lie for my personal advantage and I think, "It is okay to lie as long as it benefits me." If we apply Kant's categorical imperative to that excuse for lying, what would happen? What would happen if we allowed people to lie as long as it benefitted them? Would I want that excuse to become a universal rule for all people? Would I want all humans to think that lying is okay as long as they win somehow? The answer is no. *If we did that, then the entire notion of telling the truth would go out the window.* The entire point of telling the truth is to communicate what is actually the case. The whole notion of truth dies if we allow lying for one's selfish advantage. Or, assume that I've had a difficult life and I think, "I should kill myself because my life has been difficult." Would we want to make that into a universal rule for all people? Would we want to tell everyone that they can commit suicide just because their life has been tough? Kant would say no.

It is important to clarify what was just said. Kant is not asking us if we would like to live in a world where people can lie and commit suicide. Some of you reading this book might think, "I'd be okay living in a world where people can lie and commit suicide." That is not what Kant is doing by using the categorical imperative. He is not asking our opinion on the matter or what we think would be an acceptable outcome. *He is saying that, logically, to allow lying for one's advantage or suicide when one is sad commits a rational contradiction. Lying contradicts truth telling. And it is an intellectual contradiction to say that you will make your life better by ending it (thus ceasing to have a life at all). Kant's ethical rule weeds out what is unethical, not based on our opinions of what type of world we want to live in (if we applied the rule to all people), but by showing how both lying and suicide (as well as a host of other immoral actions) commit logical contradictions within the imperative.*

Additionally, in Kant's system of morality, we should always treat people as ends and not merely means. In this sense, we have a bit of the golden rule. We may not use people as means without also considering them as ends. We may not use people to their detriment just to accomplish some other goal. People are the ends as well. Rational beings are not objects with which we can dispense to accomplish some higher goal; they are part of that goal.

Kant also emphasized that we must act from the right motivation, and that motivation must be duty. Just doing the right action is not enough for Kant (and, it should be noted, is inadequate for many other ethical systems). A woman who stays faithful to her rich husband (whom she hates) only so she can get his money when he dies is not acting ethically. She is staying faithful, which is the right action, but her motivation is not good, and therefore she is not acting out of rational duty. She is doing the right action, but she can't be fully ethical unless she also has the right motivation. She is also treating him as a means to the end (money) and not as an end as well.

To summarize all of this, Kant thinks that what makes an action right or wrong is whether it follows a universal, rational standard that is applicable to all people, that doesn't contradict itself, that doesn't care about the consequences, where one acts out of the proper motivation of rational duty and treats others as ends.

That's deontology so far. What do you think of Kant's system? Now it's time to see how it would address our four scenarios above.

In the first scenario, the one about hiding Jewish people in your basement in WWII, Kant would say that you may not lie. This doesn't mean that you can't think of another way to protect the Jews; it just means that lying is not permitted for Kant. If you were to say that "We should lie when it protects other people," this would fail to meet the categorical imperative and would make truth-telling something that fails to universally apply. You may be able to fight the Nazis. You may be able to distract them. There may be other solutions. But you cannot lie to them and still be acting morally. You may even decide to lie to the Nazis just to practically save the lives of the Jews. But Kant would point out that, though you did the right thing in saving the Jews, *you still acted unethically by lying*. You traded one act of wrongdoing to prevent another act of wrongdoing instead of avoiding all wrongdoing.

In the second scenario, where you are the Navy SEAL, Kant would say that you cannot kill the shepherd boy. Why is that? Well, again we bump up against his categorical imperative. Should we make the statement "You may kill an innocent civilian, who is not a criminal, as long as it helps you accomplish your mission" a universal rule for all rational beings? If so, are we not saying that is it okay to kill civilians as long as it leads to a greater outcome or goal of the military? This doesn't treat people as ends, and it would say that killing innocent people is okay based on the consequences. That is a rational contradiction for Kant. How can it be moral to immorally kill someone?

Deontology doesn't care about the end result; deontology wants us to know that the action itself should be based on rational duty. Murdering a civilian based on what they "might" do is not allowed. Could you capture the boy and let him go later? Could you leave one of your SEALs to guard the boy? Sure. There are a lot of other ways to handle the situation. But one that Kant would not allow is killing the boy who is legally innocent.

In the third scenario, the one about the evil person who will kill fifty people if you don't murder one, you can probably guess what a consistent Kantian would say. You may not murder the one lady with your bare hands. The statement "We can murder an innocent person as long as it keeps some criminal from murdering others" breaks against the unmovable rock of universal duty. We would never want to apply that universally to all people, and it would be a contradiction regarding the definition of murder if we did. *Additionally, you are not called to protect the lives of others if the only way you can do so is to unjustly murder someone yourself.* If you didn't murder the one person and the sadistic killer then murdered the fifty, it should be pointed out that *you didn't murder the fifty . . . the killer did.*

In the last scenario it is difficult to say *exactly* what Kant would have done for sure (as there are actually deontological ethicists who have tried to make a case from each side). But he most likely would have condemned the use of the nuclear bombs. Killing civilians (including women and children) to avoid a *potential* loss of life for soldiers in the future most likely fails to meet the categorical imperative, and it uses some people (the Japanese) as a means only.

The reason deontological ethics is such a powerful system is due to its rigid consistency. *Acts are right or wrong regardless of consequences.* Ethics should be pursued with the right motivation. Rational duty is what grounds a moral decision. People are not just a means but also ends. Deontological ethics is what people point to when they believe that certain rules are morally binding on all people as a system that provides universal standards of what is right and wrong.

But, as in all the systems, there are flaws. For example, how broadly should we apply the categorical imperative? What if I wanted to make the following a universal rule for all rational beings: "Anyone named Zachary Lee and who is the author of this book may steal." We see that there may be a way to manipulate how narrowly we apply examples to the rule to get away with unethical acts.

Additionally, it seems hard to decide what rules should be universal when we understand that certain situations complicate the issue. For example, if we consider the Nazi scenario from above, Kant wouldn't allow lying as a universal rule, but what if we added a qualifier to the categorical imperative like "One may lie if the lie will protect the lives of innocent people from an authority who has no right to murder innocent civilians"? Perhaps certain qualifiers could be added to whatever we think is the general rule to make it conform to the imperative.

Additionally, is it truly the case that consequences shouldn't play any rule on one's ethics? Perhaps consequences don't play the *main* role in one's ethics, but could they perhaps play some role? Most of us don't make decisions while completely ignoring the consequences. We look at the action, of course, but we also consider what follows from it.

Lastly, what do you do when two rules contradict each other? Imagine that we had two categorical imperatives. One said that a child should obey their father (assuming the father wasn't commanding them to do something unethical). The other command said that a child should obey their mother (assuming the mother wasn't commanding them to do something unethical). If one is to obey their mother and their father and each parent tells them to do contradictory things, *won't the child be breaking an ethical duty despite the fact that they are trying to do the right thing*? How can the child obey both parents if the parents have put them in a situation where they must disobey one to obey the other?

What do you think about deontology so far? Are actions universally binding regardless of consequences or not? Perhaps you disagree. If so, there is another system of ethics that is all about the consequences.

Utilitarianism

Whereas deontological ethics says that what makes something right or wrong is whether or not it conforms to universal, rational duty, there is another system that takes a very different approach. This system is called *utilitarianism*. The main proponents of this ethical system are Jeremy Bentham and John Stuart Mill. Utilitarianism is easier to understand than deontological ethics, and it is simply that *an action is ethical if it leads to the greatest good for the greatest number of people.* If an act produces more overall pleasure than pain (for the highest number of people) then that is all we mean by the term *good.* If an act produces more displeasure or pain (for the highest number of people) then that is all we mean by the term *evil.*

In this system moral actions are all about utility (hence the name) or the consequences they produce. They are not about the actions per se. In this system general *happiness* is the sine qua non of ethics. Notice that this system turns Kant on his head. Whereas Kant didn't care about the consequences, this system cares *only* about consequences. Whereas Kant didn't care if the right action lead to pleasure or pain, that is the only thing this system cares about. Whereas Kant cared about having the correct motivation, this system doesn't care about motivation but only end result.

In both systems, deontology and utilitarianism, what ethical proponents are trying to do is to find a way to make ethics objective without appealing to religion or popular opinion. They are trying to create consistent systems that could be followed by the atheist just as easily as by the religious believer. This is philosophy at its finest. Guys like Kant and Mill are trying to find a way to make what is right or wrong logically obvious to rational people without appealing to divine command theory. Whereas Kant finds this objectivity in the categorical imperative, the utilitarian finds it in a formula weighing happiness against unhappiness.

If an act causes a higher level of pleasure than pain, then it is good. If it causes more pain than pleasure, it is bad. That sounds simple enough. However, as Mill pointed out in a helpful addition to Bentham, we must not only consider the *quantity* of pleasure but its *quality* as well. Watching professional wrestling produces a level of pleasure. Finishing a PhD dissertation produces a level of pleasure. But the accomplishment of some enormous task (such as the dissertation) is a higher *type* of pleasure than watching the machismo flamboyance of Hulk Hogan or the Rock. Does drinking a beer produce the same pleasure as drinking a $10,000 bottle of Bordeaux wine? Does eating a good cheeseburger compare with the pleasure that a soldier feels when he defeats his enemy in a battle and saves his best friend's life? Surely not.

Consider this example: Would you rather be a pig that has all the biological pleasure that a pig can have, or would you rather be a brilliant human who is disappointed with life? *Would you rather be a pig satisfied or a wise man (such as Socrates, to use Mill's example) dissatisfied?* If you were the pig, imagine that you could have all the food, sleep, and sex you wanted, but you couldn't get beyond being a pig. You couldn't have deep thoughts, enjoy classical music, run for office, watch your daughter's ballet recital, or read Herman Melville's *Moby Dick*. On the other hand, if you were a dissatisfied human, you couldn't have all the base pleasures that the pig is allowed to have in this thought experiment, but you could experience a different (and higher) quality of pleasure than the pig (because the pig has a lower capacity for pleasure).

In this ethical system, one can't just consider the quality of pleasure. One also must consider how many people it will affect. In utilitarianism, you must consider the *overall* amount of pleasure or displeasure. Owning a nuclear bomb might produce a lot of pleasure for you (after all, think about how cool that would be), but the fear it causes in others might overwhelm the joy you have in possessing your weapon of mass destruction. We can't just consider individual pleasure and pain; we must consider the pleasure and pain of others.

For the most extreme utilitarians, utilitarianism is almost like a gigantic pleasure calculus or numerical grid that we can use to objectively find out if something is ethical. Imagine that aliens gave humanity a super advanced computer that told us not only how much pleasure an action caused for the person doing it but for everyone else affected by that action. In theory, you could use that computer to find out what was right or wrong. Consider legalizing prostitution, for example. We could plug that into this magical computer to find out if it would be ethical to legalize it. Some people would receive pleasure from allowing prostitution to be legalized (mainly sexual pleasure), but others would receive pain (perhaps from sexual abuse or the societal decay that would accompany prostitution). The utilitarian could, in theory, plug this into the super computer to find out if it would or would not be ethical to legalize prostitution.

How would the utilitarian answer each of our four scenarios? This question seems easy to answer. It is fine to lie to the Nazis to protect the Jews, because lying is not inherently immoral. One could make the case that more pleasure will be had by keeping people alive and lying than by telling the truth and having people murdered. So far, so good. Most of us would probably lie to protect the Jewish people from the SS regardless of our ethical system. But then the scenarios start to get a bit trickier. For the utilitarian, it is also fine to kill the young shepherd boy if you are a Navy

SEAL on this mission because more overall death and more unhappiness will come from allowing the terrorist to live (who will then go on to murder more people). The fact that you murdered a kid is of no consequence. The action is not inherently immoral. All that matters is the overall pleasure versus pain calculus. You certainly strangulate the innocent person in the third scenario because that leads to less pain and death than if the sadistic criminal kills fifty people. (One death is less unhappiness than fifty deaths, so who does the killing becomes less important.) Dropping the bombs on Japan is indeed moral as long as you can show that more people may have been killed if the US had invaded Japan or if more total unhappiness would have happened by not dropping the bombs.

One quickly sees the problems with this ethical system. It leads to some conclusions that most of us would consider inherently immoral. In three of our four scenarios, most people begin to get squeamish with the *consequences* of consequentialism. They like utilitarianism in the first example (to protect the Jews), but they don't like it in the other three. Why is that? Even in the first example we see the difficulty with utilitarianism. If what is "good" is what promotes the most happiness or pleasure, then *if you can show that more Nazis will experience a higher degree of pleasure by killing Jews than others will experience by the Jews being killed, then it is morally right to murder Jewish people.* This has always been the most difficult objection to utilitarianism.

At the end of the day some people find pleasure in things most consider evil. *If sexually assaulting a child brought more overall happiness to a society than it did pain to the child, then the utilitarian is stuck saying that children should be assaulted.* As an additional problem, how exactly do we calculate pain versus pleasure? The concept of doing an action that produces more happiness than unhappiness seems simple, but how would we ever practically know the long-term pain versus pleasure effects of enacting some new law for allowing some (previously forbidden) action? We don't actually have this magical computer that can calculate total happiness; this leads to utilitarianism working well in theory but not necessarily in practice.

The differences between Kant and Mill (deontological ethics and utilitarianism)

	Kant	Mill
Are actions right or wrong in and of themselves?	Yes	No
Are rules equally binding on everyone?	Yes	No
Should you do the right action regardless of the results?	Yes	No

Does motivation matter?	Yes	No, only results matter
What type of value do people have?	Intrinsic value	Instrumental value
What do you use to decide moral decisions?	Reason	Happiness

In each of these two opposing systems, the focus is on finding a rule that grounds other rules. Their goal is to provide some principle that we can use, apart from revealed religion, that will give us an anchor to which morality can hold. There is, however, an entirely different way of thinking about ethics that is much older than Kant or Mill. This is the ethics of Aristotle.

Virtue ethics

Our third large system is called *virtue ethics* or sometimes *aretaic ethics* (the Greek word, *aretē*, refers to "excellence"—meaning an excellence in virtue and being a moral person). *In summary, the virtue ethicist chooses to act virtuously over time, which causes them to become a virtuous person who naturally does what is right, who acts from the right motivations, and who maximizes their virtuous human potential.* The focus is more on becoming a virtuously wise person (generally) than it is on knowing what (exactly) to do in any particular thought experiment. Instead of developing a full list of dos and don'ts, this view of ethics seeks to develop the whole person into the kind of citizen who will naturally know what to do when particular issues arise.

For Aristotle, you can practice virtue just like you would practice a sport or a musical instrument. In the same way that you get better at hitting a fastball the more you practice in a batting cage, and the same way that you get better at playing the piano the more you take piano lessons, Aristotle believed that you can get better at being virtuous by practicing virtue. You can become gracious by practicing being gracious. You can become temperate by practicing temperance.

This is something that we don't often consider. We all know that if we practice shooting a basketball, over time, we will get better at making our shots. However, we often forget that the more we practice patience, the more patient we will become. The more we practice being generous, the easier it will be to be generous the next time someone needs help. The more we practice resisting lust, the better we will be at resisting lust in the future. *For Aristotle, you won't become a virtuous person by merely having a desire to be virtuous. Rather, you have to practice it.* In the same way that a new flute player is bad at playing the flute when they first begin, so we will be bad at practicing virtue when we first start trying to be virtuous. It is almost as if there is a moral "muscle memory" that you can train by practicing virtue. If you are always an anxious person, then you have, for Aristotle, *practiced* being anxious by allowing yourself to dwell on anxiety-filled thoughts. If each time you were anxious you replaced those thoughts with non-anxious thoughts, you would become less anxious over time.

Let's consider one of Aristotle's favorite examples: courage. Before one can do something truly courageous, they have to practice smaller acts of courage. Courage is not just a one-time event of trying to act like you are not scared—much like taking a shot of liquid "courage" before hitting on an attractive girl in a bar. Rather, it is a lifestyle. The only way someone could do something we would consider to be truly courageous today, such as falling on a grenade to protect his fellow soldiers, is by practicing smaller acts of courage a thousand times before then. The more you practice being courageous, the more you *naturally know what to do* when the time for courage arises.

Think about how profound that is! We often like to assume that, when the moment arises, we will rise to the level of our expectations and be truly courageous. When there is a terrorist on a plane, when someone needs our kidney for a lifesaving operation, when someone breaks into our house in the middle of the night—we like to think that we will just, all of a sudden, become courageous people. But, as the old adage goes, "we do not rise to the level of our expectations but fall to the level of our training." To really know that we will be courageous when the time comes, we have to practice overcoming smaller fears in our day-to-day lives. We have to overcome phobias, endure physical and mental pain, face our fears, and do things that make us uncomfortable. If we have not practiced being courageous in small things, we have no confidence that we will be courageous when it really counts.

But courage is just one virtue. Aristotle believes we have to have many virtues to really be virtuous. Aristotle wants to develop an entire, well-rounded person. *Without having all of the virtues, you can't fully have any of them.* Much ethical training for these well-rounded people consists in following the *golden mean*. What is the golden mean? It is the ethical mean between two unethical extremes.

Let's again use courage as an example. Being courageous is not where you are, on one end of the spectrum, a coward. We all know that if you are so scared that you do not do what is right, then you do not have courage but only cowardice. Cowardice and courage are opposites. Running away from a battle because you are scared (and not because it is a tactically advantageous retreat) is cowardice. But, on the other end of the spectrum, courage is also not where you abandon all caution and foolishly throw yourself headlong into death or defeat. Someone who charges into battle in a brazen, willy-nilly flash of glory (and is immediately killed) has committed an act of suicide, not courage. True courage lies between the two ends of cowardice, on the one hand, and brashness, on the other. Courage is the golden mean between two extremes. Courage is not where you have no fear at all (a robot cannot be courageous, for example). But it is also not where you are overcome with fear. It is where you do the right action, even when you are scared, because you've overcome so many fears that you have (over time) become a courageous person.

The golden mean is not just about courage. It is about all the virtues. For example, let's consider Aristotle's virtue of wittiness. It is a mean between being foolish and being boorish. The person who is clown or court jester is too far to one extreme. No one will ever take them seriously, and they are therefore not virtuous. However, on the other end of the spectrum, the person who cannot take a joke or who is not clever is also not virtuous. They can't respond with the appropriate humor and intellectual charm when the situation calls for it. The virtuous person is one who is witty. They can make the joke when they need to, but they are also not some drunken fool falling all over themselves. The virtue ethicist also focuses on how the truly virtuous person must act from the right motivation, must have a consistent pattern of virtue, and must walk the line between two extremes for most ethical categories.

There is something very attractive about virtue ethics because it focuses more on the whole person than some of the other systems do. But its great strength can also be a great weakness. With each of our four, hypothetical ethical scenarios above, the virtue ethicist would have trouble saying what exactly you should do. Ideally, you would be someone who had practiced virtue so much that you would be able to take into account all the data and make the right decision. But what exactly is the right decision in each particular scenario? *Virtue ethicists disagree.* Some think you drop the bomb, and others don't. Most agree you shouldn't give over the Jews to the Nazis, but some then think you have still acted immorally by lying. Many think that virtue ethics must be bolstered with an additional system that gives something such as categorical commands.

For Kant and Mill, ethics can be figured out with a rigid, logical system. The biggest downside to virtue ethics is that it often (but not always) shies away from giving hard, rigorous commands. To say it as strongly as I can, *how can you practice virtuous acts if you don't know exactly which acts are virtuous without some other rule?* To become a virtuous person (who knows if you should kill the shepherd boy, so you can also kill the terrorist) you have to practice virtuous acts like deciding whether or not you should kill the shepherd boy so you can also kill the terrorist.

Deontological ethics, utilitarianism, and virtue ethics are the big systems, but there are other, smaller systems. In addition to relativism and divine command theory, some think that ethics are simply about how we feel and base ethics in sentimentality (such as David Hume and Jean-Jacques Rousseau). Some philosophers helpfully point out that most of our ethical decisions are not made because we have logically reasoned through one of these moral systems. *Rather, we respond out of animalistic emotion.* Just get on social medial after a major cultural or political event. You will see 99% of the people responding with feeling. Most people start with a position about which they are already passionate and then adjust their system of ethics around it.

Others think that ethics should benefit only oneself; our actions shouldn't take into account other people but just what is best for us. Some people think that ethics is based on our "conscience," despite the fact that our consciences often disagree with other peoples' consciences. And others think that the only thing that makes something moral is whether or not it conforms to some society's legal code (despite the fact that many things that seem immoral are legal, such as adultery). *What each person must do is to try to find an ethical system that consistently grounds their actions without that logically leading to absurd conclusions.* This is harder to do than you would think, and it is one of the reasons why philosophers have jobs.

What do you think so far? Could you make a case for each of the three large systems? Could you make a case against each of them? The question is not "Which one do you like?" but "Which one makes the best case for ethics?"

Are all moral acts selfish?

This is a common question when studying ethics. When you do a "good" act, are you doing it purely for altruistic reasons, or are you also doing it for reasons that are selfish? Perhaps you have never thought about this before. You may have just assumed that your good acts were done with completely pure motives. When you help a little old lady across the street, do you benefit from this act of "service" in some small way? You may think that you are just doing a good deed or being a good Samaritan, but you do indeed benefit. She may give you some money, and that is a benefit. Or others may see you and think that you are a good person, and that is a benefit. Or you may post a picture of you and the old lady on social media, and that is a benefit. But even if she doesn't pay you and nobody sees you, *you still feel good about yourself* for helping her, so you've still benefitted in some small way. Even when you do something *primarily* for others, there is still an element of self-interest.

Can you think of any acts you can do that are *completely selfless?* You may think that giving money to the poor is selfless because it cost you something, but what you lose in money you gain in self-esteem; you gain in feeling good that you did the "right thing" in helping a poor person. After all, being "virtuous" feels good. If you are a religious person, you may think that you are doing good things that are selfless—for others and for God—but one of the reasons you are doing them is so that you can go to heaven or so that God will be pleased with you (which is still self-interest). *Even the martyr believes they will be rewarded and therefore cannot accomplish their martyrdom without greatly benefitting in eternity.* Would you put your faith in God if he promised you that you would go to hell if you did so? Most would not. Perhaps the religious person cares even more about self-interest (and avoiding the pain of hell) than they do about *solely* loving God.

Is it wrong then to benefit from doing a good deed? If good acts still benefit us, does that make them somehow tainted by selfishness?

There is a nuance that is greatly needed in this discussion. Perhaps it is not wrong if you benefit from doing what is right. In fact, isn't benefiting from doing what is good exactly what one would expect? For Aristotle, your happiness is directly linked to your virtue, so it's not unethical when you benefit from making the right decision. *There is a huge difference between doing something that is only self-interested versus doing something for others that happens to (as a secondary consequence) benefit you.*[14] If it is true that an action cannot be moral if it also benefits you, then we are stuck saying that there are no purely morally good actions. Most, however, are not willing to say that. Rather, we should distinguish between acts that happen to benefit us secondarily from acts that *only* benefit us or benefit us at another's expense. In this way the martyr is not being selfish by being killed for their faith just because they benefit, and the man who helps the little old lady across the street is doing something that is altruistic even though he feels good after he does it.

Ethics and nuance

What would you do, practically, in each of our four sample scenarios? When we are confronted with situations like these, we often give answers that are a bit too simplistic. We want quick, easy-fix answers that just allow us to say "yes" or "no" instead of doing the difficult task of thinking deeply. Ethics demands nuance. For example, in the scenario about hiding Jews in the basement, the issue is not "Would we hand the Jews over to the Nazis?" Rather, the question is "Have you still committed the immoral action of lying, though you made the right decision in not handing them over to be killed?" There are several things to consider. Is it a "lie" if told in this "murder-y" context or only in "normal" contexts? Surely it is not a lie when a magician does a magic trick, we tell our kids that Santa Claus exists, a guy does a "pump fake" in basketball, or an undercover cop says that he is not a cop, because these situations are all different than "normal life." Or we might wonder if truth-telling is always required when the information will be used to unrighteously hurt another. To whom do we owe the truth? Do we owe it to everyone equally? What about to false or evil leaders of a country?

Perhaps ethics should cause us to think outside the box more often than we do. Is the only option that the Navy SEALs have in this scenario to either kill the shepherd boy or let him go? What about tying up the boy, leaving one SEAL to guard him, while the rest of the team goes in to kill the terrorist? You could then let the boy go right before you flew off in a helicopter. Were our only two options in scenario 4 (the atomic bomb question) to nuke Japan or launch a mainland invasion? Were the people of Japan simply civilians or potential soldiers, considering they had sworn an oath to the emperor? In scenario 3, is there any sense in which my inaction is the cause of another's action, or is that immoral decision solely the fault of the sadistic killer? Is it moral to protect life if the only way to do so is to murder an innocent person? Can we use evil with good results, or are actions inherently good or evil?

As a helpful thought experiment, I would encourage you to think of each scenario and list out as many reasons for each side as you can. This allows you to play devil's advocate and really think through both sides adequately. Then, I would encourage you to think of other ways to solve the ethical issues. Perhaps instead of answering the Nazis' question you could play dumb, or fight back, or you could have chosen a better place to hide the Jews to begin with.

Ethics and happiness

There is a famous issue in philosophy that pertains to what is pursued in and of itself over and against things that are pursued for the sake of something else. That sounds a bit convoluted, so allow me to say it another way: *What is the ultimate goal of human action?* Toward what are we striving? Suffice it to say that the most common answer (going back to the Greeks) is that humans do what we do in order to be *happy*. Human life is about trying to find joy. That may sound simplistic, but it makes a lot of sense the more one thinks about it. Why does someone go to college? Perhaps to get a diploma, so they can get a good job when they graduate. Why do they want a good job when they graduate? Perhaps to make money. Why do they want to make money? So they can buy things. Why do they want to buy things? Because they think that will make them happy. All these other decisions were fueled by a desire for happiness.

If you want to get married, why do you want to get married? Answer: because you think it will make you happy. If you want to be single, why do you want to be single? Answer: because you think it will make you happier than being married. Why do you get up early in the morning to work at a job that you don't like? Answer: because you think that at least having a job you don't like is better (and will make you happier) than not having a job at all. Everything we do, we do because we want to be ultimately happy. In fact, even the person who commits suicide wants to be happy. *The person who commits suicide believes that whatever lies on the other end of that bullet will make them happier than continuing to live in the pain of their current life.* The hedonist who pursues sexual conquests thinks that it will make them happy. Conversely, the religious martyr believes that dying for their faith will lead to more happiness (even if that happiness is in another life).

Is happiness in some way linked to ethics? Here is a truism that modern audiences most often miss: according to the ancients, especially Aristotle, *you cannot be happy without virtue.* You may think that you would find happiness if you could just do whatever you want, *but you want things that rob you of joy and you want things that lead to sadness.* Your "want to" meter is broken. Someone who is a billionaire and has all the money, food, and friends they want (but is also a child molester) may actually hate themselves because they are not virtuous and they know they are not virtuous.

There is a very famous philosophical work by Boethius called *The Consolation of Philosophy* that deals with this very issue. Boethius had been unjustly imprisoned and was wrestling with the question of why virtuous men are miserable while evil men are happy. In the work, Lady Wisdom, philosophy herself (let's call her "Athena," if you will), shows up to comfort him. She reminds him that evil men are not ultimately happy because one cannot be happy and evil. One must have virtue to truly be happy. At the end of the day, if you know you are a terrible person, money and fame only cover a wound of increasing sorrow like a Band-Aid.

Do you agree with this? Are Aristotle and Boethius correct? Can you be happy without virtue, or is it truly needed for us to live joyful lives? If so, how might we be pursuing happiness the wrong way?

I have a friend who used to work for a very large cartel in Mexico. To be clear, he is no longer a cartel member and has been living as a law-abiding citizen for decades. He actually sold me some amazing cocaine earlier this year at a really good price . . . just kidding!

He said something to me recently that reminded me of Aristotle's discussion on virtue and happiness. He said that the cartel bosses that he worked for were actually miserable. They had more money than they could spend. They had all the beautiful women they wanted. They had huge mansions, fancy cars, private jets, and the power to kill any of their enemies with just a word and a gesture of their hand. And yet, despite having all the things we think will make us happy, my buddy said they were miserable. They lived in fear that someone would kill them or their family. They suppressed the guilt they had over the murders they had committed. They knew that, despite having it all, they were not virtuous, so they could not really be happy. Joy was just out of reach.

It may very well be the case that one cannot be happy without virtue. Ethics is not just a list of rules but might also be something linked to human flourishing. This is why the study of ethics is anything but a dry, boring, sterile subject. It may be one feature (though not the only feature) of how we can be truly happy.

Conclusion

Words like *good* and *bad* seem simple on the surface. But when we study ethics, we realize how complicated they can become. Unlike other areas of philosophy, ethics affects us in powerful and practical ways. We have to consider what makes something good or bad (if those categories even exist) and, more importantly, *can we make a good case for why we think something is good or bad.*

Ethics is linked to human happiness, feelings of self-worth, and larger standards to which we are striving. For many people, ethics is closely tied to religion and what God (or some pantheon of gods) has commanded. Religion and ethics are separate categories (there are atheists with systems of ethics), but they are closely tied throughout Western history. It is to the category of religion that we will now turn our attention.

Religion

PHILOSOPHY OF RELIGION IS different than theology. Theology is the study of God within a certain faith tradition, which seeks to harmonize and clarify what that group believes about whatever God (or gods) it serves. You can have Islamic theology, Christian theology, Hindu theology, etc. In theology, the goal is to properly understand the religious claims of a particular religion. In doing Christian theology, a pastor or priest will probably try to create an entire, coherent religious system by looking at the teachings of the Bible and by analyzing what other Christians have thought about God throughout church history. In Islamic theology, an imam will try to understand Allah in light of the Koran and by analyzing what other Muslims have thought about God throughout Islamic history. The goal in theology is to create doctrines and dogmas on every topic from who God is, to how one obtains salvation, to what is or is not ethical, to how the world will end.

But theology is very different than philosophy of religion. Philosophy of religion seeks to understand things such as the existence of God, religious experience, miracles, and others *by looking at them through a philosophical lens only.* Whereas a Jewish person might say that God exists because the Hebrew Bible tells them that he exists, a philosopher wants rational proof for God's existence that is not based upon a sacred text. Whereas a religious believer will state that miracles happen by appealing to miracles performed within their tradition or within their sacred books, a philosopher has to ask, "What is a miracle and is it logically possible?" or "How should we understand miracles as authenticating one's faith if every faith tradition claims to have them?"

Philosophy of religion is an enormous topic and, along with topics such as metaphysics, attempts to deal with some of the most important questions we can ask. It is no wonder that, throughout history, most philosophers wrestled with some conception of God (or gods) even if they were very different conceptions. People as diverse as Plato and Hegel, Plotinus and Descartes, Maimonides and Locke, Avicenna and Spinoza (to name just a few in a really long list) were all very religious. Let us dip our toe in the water of religion by looking at some philosophical defenses for the existence of God. Below we will describe some proofs and then analyze a few objections to them. I'll leave it up to the reader to decide how powerful the proofs for God (and their corresponding objections) really are.

Proofs for the existence of God

The *teleological argument* is also called the *argument from design* or, if you want to get really fancy by using Kant's terminology, the *physico-theological argument.* Teleological comes from the Greek word *telos,* which means "end," "purpose," or "goal." This argument was used by Socrates, Plato, Aristotle, the Stoics, Aquinas, Paley, Flew, et al.

When we say that something has a purpose, we must realize that "purpose" is something that exists only if there is also some powerful, *intelligent mind* that exists. We talked about this idea (and the word *teleology*) briefly in the chapter on science. We don't merely say that animals evolved; we say they evolved *in order to survive.* We give an intelligent reason why they evolved. We give a purpose. We don't merely say that a female lion mates with a strong male lion. Rather, we say that she mates with a strong male lion *so she will have strong offspring.* We give the reason for why she is, biologically, more attracted to a male lion who is strong instead of a weak or sickly alternate lion. *In explanations like these (and I could give a million more) we are not merely describing phenomena. Rather, we are using concepts that work only if there is purpose (i.e., a telos), and there is no such thing as a purpose without intelligence.*

Essentially this argument for a divine being is one that seeks to prove God's existence by showing that he must be the reason for the intelligence and design we observe in the universe. If you consider the fact that two humans can make a baby, or you consider the fact that your body heals itself when injured, or you consider the fact that your eyebrows grow upward and out to the side (to keep sweat out of your eyes), or you consider the fact that your DNA is literally a discernable code, or you consider the fact that the earth is perfect for sustaining life, you quickly begin to see all the things in the universe that appear to be more than just random chance. Could it really be the case that a tiger, with its power, hunting prowess, sense of smell, and shiny, striped coat is really just due to random chemicals combining with other random chemicals? How could something that is not intelligent (randomly moving atoms) bring forth things that are clearly intelligent (such as tigers)?

William Paley gave a famous example of this argument by giving a thought experiment involving a pocket watch on a beach:

> *Suppose I found a watch upon the ground, and it should be inquired how the watch happened to be in that place, I should hardly think . . . that, for anything I knew, the watch might have always been there. Yet why should not this answer serve for the watch as well as for [a] stone [that happened to be lying on the ground]? . . . For this reason, and for no other . . . that, if the several parts had been differently shaped from what they are . . . either no motion at all would have been carried on in the machine, or none which would have answered the use that is now served by it.*[15]

I'll reword this quote to bring it into a contemporary context: Imagine that you are walking alone on a beach, and you come across the latest smartphone. This phone connects to satellites in space. You can call, text, search the internet, pay your bills, and even video chat with someone on another continent. This phone seems to possess all the genius of human technological advancement. Would it be more reasonable to assume that the phone was designed by an intelligent designer or that it just randomly happened? Is it reasonable to think that wind, and sand, and seawater all came together so perfectly that they, by mere happenstance, created a working cell phone complete with battery, numbered buttons, GPS tracking, and the ability to take selfies? We would all think that anyone who thought the phone came about only by time plus chance was absolutely mad.

Now realize that a human hand is far more complex than a cell phone. The human brain, the central nervous system, or the Milky Way galaxy are far more complex than the piece of technology we have already recognized couldn't have been formed by sporadic time and matter. One would assume that if there were no grand, intelligent designer, then nothing in the world would look designed. Rocks floating in space would have only ever remained rocks floating in space. The flight of a bald eagle, in contrast, seems to come about only through highly tuned designing. Nature (matter) might have existed apart from God, but it wouldn't have the intelligence, purpose, and the design it appears to have.

The teleological argument is probably the most "basic" argument for the existence of a supreme being. It is the one that the average religious person will most often use if you ask them why they believe in God.

There are, however, several different critiques to this argument. The atheist will argue, like our recurring friend David Hume did, that the world seems only *partially* designed. Sure we see things that seem designed—a mother can feed her baby breastmilk even when the mother is sick and the child amazingly avoids the illness—but other things seem poorly designed: cancer, a cleft palate, tornados, rape, mosquitos, tapeworms, and the fact that men are prone to hernias because there is an opening in their abdomen above their scrotum, all seem to indicate that, if God is an intelligent designer, then the world that appears somewhat "designed" seems to severely limit his intelligence. What type of God can we assume exists if we reason solely by looking at the world?

Perhaps God exists, but logically, we could infer only that he would be as intelligent as the messed-up world that we observe. The theist will respond that God did not create the world originally with all these bad things. There was no cancer or birth defects in the garden of Eden. Rather, God created the world good, and it is due only to the influence of sin and the rebellion of mankind that God cursed the earth. The things we see that look undesigned do so only because they are corrupted, not because God originally made them that way. The atheist will respond that this commits the logical fallacy of "begging the question." *To assume that the world is broken because of sin already assumes God's existence, which is the very thing one is supposed to be proving with the teleological argument.*

If God is truly all-powerful and truly doesn't need anything he creates to make him more glorious (because he supposedly has been infinitely glorious for all eternity), couldn't he have made things better than they are and still retained his original glory? Couldn't there be one less rape than there is? Couldn't there be one less war, economic collapse, or pandemic?

In his *Dialogues Concerning Natural Religion* Hume points out that if we are supposed to infer a creator by looking at creation, then we don't come up with anything like the Judeo-Christian view of God. In nature we see plurality; that doesn't allow us to conclude that there is a singular, monotheistic

God. In nature we see what is limited; that doesn't allow us to conclude that there is an unlimited God. In nature we see things that are ugly; that doesn't allow us to conclude that there is a beautiful God. In nature we see things that are finite; that doesn't allow us to conclude that there is an infinite God.

Additionally, we can prove only that the universe *looks designed, not that it is actually designed.* The universe is not like a pocket watch or a cell phone. We don't have anything else to which we can compare it. We basically assume that we, as humans, know what looks designed in our own lives and then read this onto God. Hume states:

> *The curious adapting of means to ends, throughout all nature, resembles exactly, though it much exceeds, the productions of human contrivance; of human designs, thought, wisdom, and intelligence. Since, therefore, the effects resemble each other, we are led to infer, by all the rules of analogy, that the causes also resemble; and that the Author of Nature is somewhat similar to the mind of man, though possessed of much larger faculties, proportioned to the grandeur of the work which he has executed. By this argument a posteriori, and by this argument alone, do we prove at once the existence of a Deity, and his similarity to human mind and intelligence.*[16]

Additionally, the atheist will say that, even if the teleological argument were true, it would prove only that some intelligent being existed. It would not prove that there was only one God or that he possessed the attributes attributed to him in organized religion. The theist will respond by saying that this objection misses the point of the proof. The proof is simply to show that one cannot be an atheist (i.e., that there is *some* divine being). One can work out which divine being (and what they are like) after one has consented to the fact that at least one exists.

What do you think about this first argument for God's existence? If you think it is a good argument, how do you account for the things that appear to be undesigned or to the charge that this proves only that there is some Creator, not that it is the God of organized religion? If you think the argument is a bad one, how do you account for things that seem to have purpose and design if everything is merely random atoms bumping into each other?

But the teleological argument is merely the simplest argument for God's existence. There are many other arguments that we must consider.

The *moral argument*, sometimes called the *axiological argument*, is an argument for God's existence based on universal morality. The argument goes something like this: Humans intrinsically have a sense of right and wrong. Yes, some cultures will let you kill people for things that other cultures will not. Yes, some cultures allow you to have more than one sexual partner, and others do not. But there is no culture that believes that anyone can murder anyone else anytime they want without reason. There is no culture that says anyone can sexually assault anyone else they want anytime they want. There is some universal standard of morality that seems to be based on more than mere opinion.

It's not the case that, if you assault my wife, I think you have merely done something that displeased me (as if morality were based soley on my opinion). Nor is it that I think your assault is condemned only because it is frowned upon by the larger culture (as if morality were based soley on public opinion). Rather, it seems like you have objectively done something that is bad. Even the moral relativist (deep down) thinks that white supremacy is bad. Even the moral relativist (deep down) thinks assaulting a child is bad. Even a moral relativist (deep down) thinks experimenting on Jews at Auschwitz is bad. Why do we have such a strong sense of inherent morality? Yes, there are always crazy psychopaths who don't have a conscience, but, on the whole, this sense of morality is quite ubiquitous. As author C. S. Lewis says:

> *Whenever you find a man who says he does not believe in real Right and Wrong, you will find the same man going back on this a moment later. He may break his promise to you, but if you try to breaking one to him he will be complaining "It's not fair" before you can say "Jack Robinson." A nation may say treaties do not matter; but then, next minute, they spoil their case by saying that the particular treaty they want to break was an unfair one. But if treaties do not matter, and if there is no such thing as Right and Wrong—in other words, if there is no Law of Nature—what is the difference between a fair treaty and an unfair one?[17]*

According to this argument, when we say something is right or wrong, we are saying that it conforms to the larger category of what is objectively *Right* (capital *R*) or objectively *Wrong* (capital *W*). Even thieves think it is wrong when someone steals from them. Even murderers think it is wrong when someone tries to murder them. In fact, even pirates, who would rape, murder, and pillage had their own pirate code of rules they would not break. According to the Pirate Code of Bartholomew Roberts in 1722:

> *Every man shall be called fairly in turn by the list on board of prizes, because over and above their proper share, they are allowed a shift of clothes. But if they defraud the company to the value of even one dollar in plate, jewels, or money, they shall be marooned. If any man rob another, he shall have his nose and ears slit, and be*

> *put ashore where he shall be sure to encounter hardships. . . . If any*
> *man shall be found seducing one of the latter sex [women] and*
> *carrying her to sea in disguise, he shall suffer death. . . . None shall*
> *strike another on board the ship, but every man's quarrel shall be*
> *ended onshore by sword or pistol.*[18]

Of course, as in all these proofs, there are critiques of the argument. Just because people think something is wrong doesn't make it objectively wrong. *All you can prove is that most cultures think something is wrong, not that it objectively is.* Even if you could show that everyone thought murder was wrong, that doesn't mean that it *objectively* is; it only means that everyone agrees that it *subjectively* is. People can be universally incorrect (like when most of the population thought the Earth was flat), and this applies to morality as well. This argument might get the proof entirely backwards: *Is it the case that universal assent is due to there being an objective standard of morality, or do we think there is a universal standard of morality because it has universal assent?*

Perhaps we have a universal sense of morality because, due to evolution, we developed practices to protect our species (such as a revulsion to murder). We may feel shame when we do something wrong, but your dog also seems to feel shame when it goes to the bathroom on the carpet.

Lastly, is the central claim of this proof even true? It seems that there are many ethical issues where cultures have strongly disagreed. Whether homosexuality should be allowed, how many wives you can have, and whether pride was a virtue or a vice are all issues that have had varying answers across cultures in world history. Even something we think of as universally condemned (such as murder) doesn't hold for the tribes in South America (who would decapitate people each day to make sure the sun came up the next morning); or for the Spartans (who would practice murdering slaves to prepare for battle); or for tribes who cannibalized their enemies.

The next two proofs for God's existence appear to have a stronger philosophical foundation than the teleological or moral arguments. This is due to the fact that they build a logical case for God's existence from the ground up instead of appealing to things that are more amorphous (such as our conceptions about design and morality). This doesn't mean that they will or won't persuade you. But it should be noted that their approach is more philosophical than the "commonsense" approach of the above two arguments.

The *cosmological argument* (from the Greek word *cosmos*, which means "world" or "universe") is an argument that states that God is the first cause of everything else that is. God is the "unmoved mover" that begins the entire sequence of cause and effect in the universe. Major proponents of this argument include Plato, Aristotle, Maimonides, Anselm, Aquinas, Duns Scotus, Descartes, Spinoza, Leibniz, Locke, et al.

If you think about it, everything going on in the universe is related to cause and effect. What is the cause of me typing this sentence on my computer? It is the fact that my computer has power. Why does my computer have power? It is because it has a full battery. How did it get a full battery? It is because I plugged it into the electrical outlet. On and on I could go back to the very beginning of time. But this leads us to ask, "What is that first cause?" If we have an entire chain of cause and effect, what is it that began this chain?

You may be tempted to say that this sequence of cause and effect just goes backwards forever. Perhaps there was no "start" to the universe; perhaps the universe has always existed. The cause of me is my parents. The cause of them is their parents. The cause of them was their parents. (And we could keep going backwards to before the big bang.) But here is the problem with thinking that way. *If the causal chain goes back forever, then how the heck did we get to today?* If the universe is eternal and the cause and effect chain goes backwards forever, then we would have had to traverse an infinite amount of time (and causes) to get to today. But here we are . . . today. Ergo, the universe cannot be eternal. There must be something that started the process, since it cannot have gone on forever.

You may be tempted to say, "But then wouldn't God run into this same problem if he has always existed?" If the universe can't be eternal, then why does God get to be eternal and not run into the exact same problem? The theist will point out that God is not like the universe. The universe contains matter and is therefore part of the space-time continuum. God, though, is not material. He is outside the bounds of space and time. God can exist forever—no problem. It is only the universe that cannot be eternal. Without God there is nothing that would have started the whole chain of events that is itself not a part of that chain. As the medieval philosopher Thomas Aquinas says:

> *Because effects always depend on some cause, and a cause must exist if its effect exists . . . it is therefore impossible that, in the same manner and in the same way, anything should be both the one which effects a change and the one that is changed. . . . We do not find that anything is the efficient cause of itself. Nor is this possible, for the thing would then be prior to itself, which is impossible.*[19]

Refuting the cosmological argument is difficult. One can say that the universe has always existed, but we saw how that runs into a contradiction whether you are discussing time or causation. One can say that the universe started itself, but I'm not sure what that would even mean (or how the universe could be prior to itself to even begin to start itself). One could point out that this only shows that a nonphysical, eternal being started the universe but not that this being is God (though the most common definition of God is indeed a nonphysical, eternal being), so I'm not sure that this objection works either. One can say this doesn't show that the God of a particular faith tradition exists, only that some God exists. But (again) the theist is trying to prove only that there is a God—one can discuss which God it is after their opponent has conceded that there must be at least one.

The best attempt at refuting the argument comes again from the congenial atheist David Hume. Hume would say that the idea that "every event has a cause" is true if we are talking about things *inside* the universe, but it is a category mistake to apply it to the universe *as a whole*. To say that everything has a cause, and then to jump to the conclusion that the whole system (the whole universe) itself has a cause, seems to be a slippery logical move.

To say that one domino knocks over a second domino, which in turn knocks over a third domino is completely reasonable. Dominoes are individual things within the "system." But then to conclude that therefore everything that exists (as an entire and universal system) has to have a cause seems to commit a logical fallacy. Just because we see cause and effect within the system, what reason do we have for thinking that the system as a whole must have a cause? Does this rejoinder refute the cosmological argument? Even if you began with the concept of the universe, you would need something to start the sequence of cause and effect *inside* that universe. You would also run into the problem of how the universe as a whole could be eternal if it contains matter that would then have to be infinitely old (whatever that means). Can you separate the system from the things that make up the system, or are they integrally linked?

Some opponents of the cosmological argument will show that the common notion of God creating a universe out of nothing (Latin: *ex nihilo*) doesn't make any sense. Aristotle, for example, held that the universe was indeed eternal and gave many strong proofs for it (though he also thought there was an "unmoved mover"). Perhaps one can refute the cosmological argument by showing that its opposite (the universe coming into being) is impossible. How does God bring something forth out of nothing (as *nothing* is not a substance or a thing from which other things can be brought forth)? The popular philosophical slogan *ex nihilo nihil fit* (out of nothing comes nothing) was a common objection given by pagans to the Christian notion of creation.

What do you think of the cosmological argument. If you think it is a strong argument, why is that? If you think it can be refuted, why is that? Is the universe eternal? If so, how did we get to today? If you think God created it, how?

Perhaps the logically strongest, but least practically persuasive, of the arguments for God's existence is the *ontological argument*. The biggest proponent of this argument is St. Anselm of Canterbury. In fact, it wasn't called the ontological argument originally (that is a name given to it by Kant). Rather, it was called the *argumentum anselmi* (Anselm's argument). Anselm was not the only one to use this argument. Many philosophers, both from the past (such as René Descartes) and the present (such as Alvin Plantinga), have their own versions of the argument.

Anselm defines God as *a being greater than which none can be thought.* If God is a being who has all the perfections (think of a perfection as a positive, good quality) to the highest degree—he possesses the highest level of goodness, the highest level of love, the highest level of intelligence, etc.— then he would have to possess the perfection of existence to the highest degree as well. Anselm says:

> *If that than which a greater cannot be thought can be thought of as not existing, this very thing than which a greater cannot be though is not that than which a greater cannot be thought. But this is contradictory. . . . But how did he [the fool who denies God's existence] manage to say in his heart what he could not think? Or how is it that he was unable to think what he said in his heart?*[20]

That sounds confusing, so allow me to elaborate further.

Pretend for a second that I promised to give you a unicorn as a gift. You are probably skeptical about my ability to give you a unicorn, so I'll go ahead and give you one just to prove that I can. Close your eyes for a moment and think of a unicorn. There you go! I just gave you a unicorn. I gave you a unicorn *made of thoughts*. I gave you a unicorn that existed in your mind. But wait a second . . . that's not what you were expecting. Surely my gift would be much better if I actually gave you a unicorn in reality and not just in your mind. What does this little thought experiment have to do with anything? *It simply proves that something that actually exists in reality is better than something that exists only in your mind.* Hang on to this notion for a second because we will come back to it.

Step 1: Think of a being that is so great that you cannot possibly think of a greater being (i.e., "God").

(Note: If this being is the greatest, then it means that this being would have every desirable quality to the highest degree. This being would have love to the highest degree, justice to the highest degree, strength to the highest degree, etc.)

Step 2: Ask yourself this question: "Would this being be better if it existed in reality or just in my mind?"

(Well, like the unicorn example, something is better if it exists in reality and not just in your mind.)

Conclusion: Therefore, this most perfect being (God) must exist in reality and not just in your mind.

To say it another way:

1. If you can think of a being so great that you cannot think of a better one

and

2. If it is better for that being to exist in reality than to just exist in your mind

then

3. God must exist in reality and not just in your mind.

Now, I know what you're thinking: "That can't be right. Are you saying that just because I can think of a really good thing in my mind, then it must also exist in reality?" Actually, no. You've misunderstood the argument.

The argument is not saying that just because you can think of a really great thing, that thing must exist. The argument is saying that if you say you can think of a being who is so great that you cannot think of a greater one and then you say this being exists only in your mind, *then you have contradicted yourself* because you *can* actually think of a greater one, namely, one that exists in reality and *not just* in your mind.

To say it another way: For Anselm, you can't actually think of God as not existing. When you try to do that, you are not really thinking about God. Thinking of God as not existing is like trying to think of a square circle or thinking of two plus two equaling five. God is not a being who can either exist or not exist (like a cat). God is a being who necessarily exists by definition. The ontological argument is an argument that says that the idea of a non-existing-most-perfect-being is a logical contradiction. If you are thinking about a God who might not exist, you are not really thinking about God. *If you are thinking about the best thing but also thinking that best thing might not exist, then you are not thinking about the best thing.* Descartes says:

But granted I can no more think of God as not existing than I can think of a mountain without a valley, nevertheless it surely does not follow from the fact that I think of a mountain with a valley that a mountain [actually exists]. . . . Likewise, from the fact that I think of God as existing, it does not seem to follow that God exists. . . . From the fact that I am unable to think of a mountain without a valley, it does not follow that a mountain or valley exists anywhere, but only that, whether they exist or not, a mountain and a valley are inseparable from one another. But from the fact that I cannot think of God except as existing, it follows that existence is inseparable from God, and that for this reason he really exists. Not that my thought brings this about or imposes any necessity on anything; bur rather the necessity of the thing itself, namely of the existence of God, forces me to think this. For I am not free to think of God without existence, that is a supremely perfect being without a supreme perfection, as I am to imagine a horse with or without wings.[21]

In philosophy we often talk about what are called *possible worlds*. By possible worlds, we are not talking about scientific dimensions or alternate universes or anything "sci-fi." In philosophy, a possible world is simply a logical way the universe could have been. We are not saying that other possible worlds actually exist. It is just a shorthand way of talking about how the world might have been. For example, I could have been named Jack instead of Zach. In philosophy we would say that there is a possible world in which Zach is named Jack. We are not saying that world actually exists anywhere; we are just saying that the world could have been that way. I could have had red hair instead of brown hair. That is a possible world. I could have a pet turtle. That is a possible world. There is almost an infinite number of possible worlds.

However, there is no possible world (or a way the world could have been) that allows for two plus two to equal five. There is no possible world in which there are married bachelors. There is no possible world that contains square circles. All this is to say that there are a lot of ways that the world could have been *but none that can contain logical contradictions.*

"What does this have to do with the ontological argument?" you ask. If there is a possible world that contains a being who must exist in every possible world, then that being does indeed exist in every possible world, including the real world. To say it another way: if it is possible that a necessary being might exist, then that being does indeed (necessarily) exist in all possible worlds. To say it a third way: if there is a possible scenario where there is a being-who-exists-in-every-possible-scenario, then that being does indeed exist in every possible scenario.

I realize that I have spent more time on this argument than the others because this one is the most "philosophical" of the arguments and students are most apt to misunderstand it. Please allow me one more clarifier before we venture into a possible refutation. The idea of "nothingness" may be a logical contradiction. Pause for a moment and try to think of absolute nothingness. You actually can't do it. If you are thinking of anything at all, you are not thinking of nothingness. When most people try to think of nothingness they just think of a vast, black space. But that is not thinking of nothingness. Rather, you are thinking of vastness, blackness, and space. Some theologians and philosophers have pointed out that nothingness is a contradiction. There must be something that exists and exists necessarily, and this is God. The eighteenth-century theologian and philosopher Jonathan Edwards says:

> *That there should absolutely be nothing at all is utterly impossible. The mind can never, let it stretch its conceptions ever so much, bring itself to conceive of a state of perfect nothing. . . . Indeed, we can mean nothing else by "nothing" but a state of absolute contradiction. And if a man thinks that he can think well enough how there should be nothing, I'll engage that what he means by "nothing" is as much something as anything that ever [he] thought of in his life. . . . So that we see it necessary some being [i.e., God] should eternally be.*[22]

Can the ontological argument be refuted? It seems to contain only true premises, has a valid structure, and appears to be sound. The most famous supposed refutation comes from Kant. Kant believed that the argument fails because "being cannot be predicated." He says:

> *But if we wish to think existence through the pure category alone, then we must not be surprised that we cannot indicate any mark whereby to distinguish existence from mere possibility.*[23]

Let's perform a thought experiment to understand what Kant is saying. In your mind, think of a red ball that exists in your living room. Now, once you have done that, think of the ball as getting bigger. Now think of the red ball as changing into the color blue. Now think of the ball as having white stripes. In each of these examples, we are saying something new about the ball (which is called *predicating*—predicating is when you say something about something). In each of these examples, your thought of the ball changed when we predicated something new about it. Each of these predicates changed your mental image of the ball.

Let's start over and try the experiment again. Think of a red ball in your room, and now imagine that it exists. Notice, this last predicate was not like the other ones. In each of the other predicates, the image in your mind changed. But, when you imagined a red ball and then imagined that it does indeed exist, *nothing changed in your mind regarding the thought of the ball. Being or existence is not something that you can predicate about the ball (like its size or color).* We already assume the ball's existence whenever we are talking about it. Kant believes this is the fallacy that the ontological argument makes: *it assumes that existence is a perfection, like goodness, even though existence is already presupposed in the argument.*

Is Kant right? Some think so, but others do not. Some think that existence is indeed a predicate. A unicorn existing and a unicorn not existing may be more than merely a verbal distinction. We certainly won't solve this issue here. My goal is only to present a bit of a back-and-forth for each argument.

Which arguments are more persuasive to you, and why? Or, if you don't think any of them are persuasive, how would you deal with each one (and replace it with a better counterargument)?

There are many other arguments that people use to prove the existence of God. Everything from historical records to eyewitness testimony are used by people to try to prove (or disprove) the existence of a divine being. However, this leads us to an important question. If God does exist, does he even want people to believe in him because of logical proofs? Could God possibly want people to trust him by faith instead? Is conversion to some religion a spiritual thing or merely an intellectual process whereby someone reasons well enough to come to a knowledge of God? Even if God did exist, it might not be the case that the way he wants humans to come to know him is through philosophical proofs. Perhaps it is through belief in divine revelation, an experience of the divine, or though conversations with his followers that God (if he exists) prefers to be known.

Academics have come up with additional attempts to prove God's existence, and though most of them are subsets of these primary four arguments, there are some that are indeed unique.

George Berkeley

Some philosophers have come up with ingenious systems of philosophy that require God to be part of the picture. We have already looked briefly at Leibniz's view of monads. For Leibniz, different substances don't causally interact (because one substance cannot affect an entirely different substance). Rather, *it is God* who preestablishes everything that every substance (i.e., monad) will do, and everything moves according to God's predesigned plan. Another figure, George Berkeley, believed that his system solved the problems in philosophy by requiring that God be the divine mind in which everything was perceived. In a sense, everything is an idea in the mind of God. That sounds a bit abstract, so let's pause to elaborate upon this metaphysical (and religious) system.

A problem that has bedeviled philosophers for centuries is how the mind and the body interact (see the chapter on the mind-body problem for more info). In short, the question is "How can something that is not material (mind/soul) interact with things that are material (body)?" How can it be that ideas and matter interact if they are so different in their essence? After all, if I ask you how much an idea weighs, you won't be able to give me an answer, because an idea itself (not merely the chemicals in the brain) is not made of matter; it has no weight. Berkeley's solution is simple, but it offends common sense. *Berkeley would say that everything is idea and that matter doesn't exist.*

That sounds backwards to most modern, science-loving Americans. If anything, most of us are probably inclined to say that humans don't have an immaterial part of us (soul or mind) but are merely material bodies with material brains. But Berkeley takes the opposite view. The way that ideas and matter can interact is by simply getting rid of the matter. *Everything is idea.*

Follow me closely, because many people misunderstand Berkeley. He is not saying that we are just in a dream or that things are not real or that we don't feel hard things with our senses. You cannot just walk up to a podium and kick it to try to refute Berkeley. He is much too smart for that. What he is saying all depends on his definitions of idea and matter. *By* idea *he means something that is perceived by a mind. By* matter *he means something that is not perceived by a mind.* We like to think that a table in our kitchen just exists by itself and that it would still exist if all the humans instantly vanished from the earth. But why do we think that? The only table we've ever known in our kitchen has always been a *perceived table*; it has always been one that we could see or feel. It has always been a table perceived by some mind. There is never just a table that exists in the room; rather, I *perceive* the table by using my senses, which send the info to my mind, and that table I see in my mind is the one that exists.

What Berkeley does is to shift the burden of proof. The burden of proof is not on Berkeley to prove that the things we think exist are perceived by our minds (everyone agrees with that). *The burden of proof is on the person who thinks there is this mysterious stuff that could exist even if nobody ever perceived it (called matter), despite the fact that everything we think exists (and everything we think is made of matter) has been perceived by our minds.*

After all, if there is indeed unperceived stuff called matter, then how on earth do we know it exists? After all, everything we think we can see is something that has been seen! Pause for a moment and try to think of something that is made of matter that no one has ever perceived—something that has never gone through the grid of someone's (or something's) mind. You can't do it. Everything you think is made of matter has been perceived (either by you or another), thus making it fit Berkeley's definition of an *idea*. When you are looking at a table (which you think is made of matter), the fact that you are perceiving it at that moment only proves that you have an idea of the table; the image is received through your senses, and you have a picture of it in your mind. If things existed unperceived, then how could you ever prove that thesis? As soon as you tried to prove that unperceived things exist, you would have to perceive them—thus making them a perceived idea.

Have you ever heard the question "If a tree falls in the forest and nobody is around to hear it, does it still make a sound?" That question is related to Berkeley's thesis. We like to think that it would make a sound, but as soon as you ask, "Why do you think it would still make a sound?," you are stuck saying, "Because when I've heard trees fall in the past, they made a sound." But as soon as you say that sentence, you are appealing to something perceived (i.e., "hearing," in this case) from your past to prove the tree made a sound. That wasn't the question. The question was whether or not the tree made a sound when it was *unperceived* by anyone (i.e., pure "matter"). *You are essentially saying that you know that a tree makes a sound because you perceived it, but you think it still makes a sound when nobody perceives it.* But you have tripped over your own logical feet. Berkeley would point out that all you've proved is that perceived falling trees make sounds, not unperceived falling trees.

Where does God come into the picture for Bishop Berkeley? Everything is an idea, and if it is not being perceived by a human mind, *it still exists as a perceived thing because God's divine mind is perceiving everything all the time.* To be is to be perceived (*esse est percipi*).

There is a famous limerick related to Berkeley's thesis by Ronald Knox:

> *There was a young man who said, "God*
> *Must find it exceedingly odd*
> *To think that the tree*
> *Should continue to be*

When there's no one about in the quad."

"Dear Sir: Your astonishment's odd;
I am always about in the quad.
And that's why the tree
Will continue to be
Since observed by, Yours faithfully, God."[24]

In a nutshell, Berkeley finds a way to solve how different substances can interact by showing that they are actually made up of the same substance—idea. We never encounter unperceived "matter" but perceive things in our minds (what he calls "ideas"). When we are not perceiving something, God is perceiving it all the time. That is how we know that our kitchen table doesn't disappear when we are no longer looking at it. God is always looking at it.

What do you think of Berkeley's thesis? If you like it, where could it go wrong? If you don't like it, how do you refute it? Berkeley's notion, though it undoes common sense, is terribly difficult to disprove. But you have to hand it to him. If he is right, he has solved one of the most basic problems in metaphysics and has used God to do it.

Berkeley is not the only one who gives additional proofs for God. There are many. The point of this section is to show that religion and philosophy, far from being enemies, are often reliant on one another. Some philosophers, however, think that you can believe in God even if you never gave a rational proof for his existence. They state that belief in God is the starting point, not an end point, for inquiry.

God as a properly basic belief

Some philosophers and theologians don't think it is the job of the theist to prove God's existence at all. They think that shifts the burden of proof. They will point out that belief in God is perfectly rational (which is why almost every major culture in world history has been religious). They will say that we, as humans, start with belief in God. It is a properly basic belief. In the same way I don't have to prove that I'm not in a dream right now, I also don't have to prove that God exists. I can just begin with that belief. Contra Descartes, we can know some things even if we don't start with a notion of absolute certainty. We know a great many things despite the fact that we *could* be wrong. Some things we know intrinsically. John Calvin, the leader of the Protestant Reformation in Geneva, points to an intrinsic *sensus divinitatis* (sense of the divine):

> *Therefore, since from the beginning of the world there has been no region, no city, in short, no household, that could do without religion, there lies in this a tacit confession of a sense of deity inscribed in the hearts of all. . . . From this we conclude that it is not a doctrine that must first be learned in school, but one of which each of us is master from his mother's womb and which nature itself permits no one to forget.*[25]

If God does indeed exist, then to pretend like he doesn't would be intellectually dishonest. One cannot step away from the truth of God's existence and then act as though they can prove it. What both the theist and the atheist do is pretend like they can actually put aside the most important beliefs they have and then step into an assumption-less mental octagon to fight it out. But that is impossible. If God does exist, then to even pretend like he doesn't (for the sake of argument) would be to step away from the thing that is true to try to prove it is true. And if God does not exist, to pretend like he does would also be to step away from the truth. As one philosopher of religion, Cornelius Van Til, says:

> *All reasoning is, in the nature of the case, circular reasoning. The starting-point, the method, and the conclusion are always involved in one another.*[26]

Perhaps it would be better to admit that we all have presuppositions that we cannot put aside. The Christian should argue with the beginning presupposition that God does exist. The atheist should argue with the beginning presupposition that God does not exist. After they have each made their case for their entire worldview, we can then look at both arguments and see where the flaws and weak points may lie. The view with the fewer problems wins. Of course, the theist will think their worldview has fewer weak points, and the atheist will think their worldview has fewer weak points. But, logically and objectively, one side must have a stronger argument than another.

What do you think about this point? If God does exist, then does one have to prove his existence, or would that be the starting point? If God does not exist, then does one have to prove that he doesn't exist, or would that be the starting point? On whom does the burden of proof lie? It seems to all depend on who is right, but that is the very thing we are trying to determine. Philosophy of religion can be tricky.

God and evil

A common topic within the philosophy of religion is the nature of evil. If God exists and is supposed to be all-powerful and wholly and totally good, then why is there evil in the world? As our frequent companion Hume would say:

> Is God willing to prevent evil, but not able? Then he is not omnipotent. Is he able, but not willing? Then he is malevolent. Is he both able and willing? Then whence cometh evil? Is he neither able nor willing? Then why call him God?[27]

This topic is called *theodicy*, from the Greek words for God (*theos*) and justice (*dikē*). Theodicy is an attempt to vindicate divine goodness and providence in view of the existence of evil. Evil poses quite a problem within a theological system, especially a system such as the Judeo-Christian/Islamic notion of an omnipotent, omni-benevolent, eternal God. If God exists (and he is supposed to be good), then why does he allow the Holocaust, child molestation, infanticide, wars, terrorism, cancer, and rape?

There are several attempts to answer this question. Some of them are more persuasive than others. The first attempt is simply to deny that God exists. The reason there is evil in the world is because there is no God (or gods). That sounds simple enough, but that opens a Pandora's box of problems related to evil. If God doesn't exist, then we may not even be able to say that there is any evil in the world at all. *Without an objective standard of good, then how do we know that some things are objectively evil and not merely things we "don't like"?* In one sense, it would seem odd to not believe in God due to the existence of evil in the world, because when you get rid of God, you get rid of evil as an objective meta-category as well. Additionally, if evil isn't objective, then neither is good. If evil is based just on utilitarianism (as discussed in the chapter on ethics) or on cultural opinion, then nothing might be objectively good either. As the sixth-century philosopher Boethius says:

> We cannot raise the question "How can there be evil if God exists?" without raising the second: "How can there be good if He exists not?"[28]

So the atheist is inclined to say that God doesn't exist because there is *evil* in the world, but this ignores the counterargument: "God must exist because there is *good* in the world." If we are going to think of evil as objective (and as proof against a divine being), then we should also think of good as objective and proof for a divine being.

Another way to try to deal with the problem of evil is simply to deny that God is good. It could be the case that there is an all-powerful being who is evil or who directly does evil. That solves the problem of evil in the world, but it leads to a pretty terrifying conclusion. In this possibility, the solution is worse than the problem. Most philosophers throughout history have not believed in an all-powerful, evil God (though it is a logical possibility).

A third option in dealing with theodicy is to deny that God is all-powerful. This is exactly the answer given in many polytheistic systems. In Greek mythology, the "gods" can't prevent evil, because they are more like super humans than gods. Perhaps an evil god is stronger than one of the good gods, and that is why there is evil in the world. They simply lack the power to keep evil from happening or lack the power to control humans. This answer, however, won't do if one has a concept of an all-powerful God. God, in most versions of monotheism, is explicitly said to be all-powerful and even sovereign over evil.

Another option is, of course, to just deny that evil exists. We could formulate a religious system where things "just happen" or where goodness is subjective. That would solve the theodicy issue but at quite a cost. Are we really willing to say that the Holocaust was not evil but, rather, just unfortunate?

In each of these potential "solutions" above, we have simply denied one of the following ideas:

1. God is all-powerful.

2. God is all-good.

3. Evil exists.

The first solution we discussed denied numbers 1 and 2 (because it said God didn't exist at all). The second solution denied number 2 (that God is all-good). The third solution denied number 1 (that God is all-powerful). And the last solution denied number 3 (that evil exists).

Most people, however, are not satisfied with these solutions because they end up with a weak God, an evil God, no God at all, or no objective evil. *They want to know if these three ideas can exist in tension or if they are actually contradictory.* So, philosophers of religion have come up with some better potential solutions to the problem of evil.

The first is called the *free will defense* and it has a long and illustrious history. It basically states that God was not free to create humans—who truly had a free will—without also allowing the possibility of evil. Unless God created humans to be robots who simply did what they must do, then God had to allow real choice. For there to be real choice, God had to allow the possibility of evil. In this solution, God exalts human freedom as more important than having a perfect universe.

The problems with the free will defense, of course, are numerous. First, it doesn't seem like being able to choose to do evil is what makes one free or else God himself is not free (for he supposedly cannot do evil). The free will defense doesn't account for nonmoral evil or chaos that seems to occur occurs in nature even outside of Earth (such as the chaos of the constant red storm on the planet Jupiter). In many faith traditions, God is sovereign over the wills of men, so the free will defense may limit the power of God. And, most damningly, even if God couldn't tamper with man's "free will," he would at least have known what humans would have chosen. Why didn't God choose someone he knew would have used their free will to choose what is good? If he knows Adam and Eve will eat of the forbidden fruit, why not choose Jessica and Steve, whom he knew would have chosen to obey God instead? If God knows the devil is going to trick humanity, then why just not create him to begin with?

Another defense that is given to the problem of evil is that God had to allow evil to show how good he is. In the same way that a flashlight shines more brightly in a dark room than in the sunshine, and in the same way that a tapestry is more beautiful if the bright reds and greens are set on a dark background, so God had to allow evil so that we might better see how good he really is. Perhaps God allowed evil to contrast with his goodness.

The problems with this line of reasoning are also abundant. First, this makes it sound like God needed evil to be glorious. But God, if he exists, is already supposed to be infinitely glorious and to need nothing. Second, though it is true that we humans might see God's goodness better against a dark background of evil, in most theological systems God doesn't make decisions based on what humans will or will not think about him. Rather, he makes them based on his sovereign good pleasure to do what he wants. Furthermore (at least in a common Christian scheme), this would mean that God was not as glorious before mankind sinned or that angels didn't get to see him as glorious before the supposed fall from paradise. Lastly, are we really willing to say that God allows evil just so we will better appreciate it when good things happen? Would you kick your child and then give them candy so they would see how great the candy was compared to the abuse?

In concluding this section I'd like to offer two of the better answers, in my opinion, to the problem of evil. This does not mean I either do or do not believe them. Rather, it is simply to state that they give better answers than the supposed solutions above.

The first is that God could use evil for an ultimately good purpose. When we think of evil, we usually isolate our conception of evil to one particular instance or act. However, we don't often ask if that seemingly evil action will lead to a good outcome in the future. *This defense basically says that the problem of evil is a problem only if God doesn't have a good reason for why he ordains it.* If he has a reason for it (even if we don't know what that reason is), then the concepts of God being good, God being powerful, and evil being in the world are not contradictory.

A knife can be used to cut someone for an evil purpose (such as murder), or a knife can be used to cut someone for a good purpose (such as when a surgeon uses one to perform surgery to save one's life). We can't just look at the cut or the knife and judge it to be good or bad; we have to look at *why* the cut is being made. What is the *purpose* of the cut? What is the purpose of the knife? Is it to murder or to heal? Perhaps this is how God uses evil. If this is the case, then there may be a way that he is still good (because he has an ultimately good purpose and because God himself does not directly do the evil—it is always done by secondary agents), and that he is still powerful (because he is sovereignly directing the event toward an ultimate goal). If I were to ask you if it is unloving for me to push someone, you might say yes. But if I were pushing them out of the way of an oncoming train, you would see that (in a larger context) my action was actually loving.

Lastly, there is an argument, popularized by the philosopher Augustine of Hippo, that explains that *God did not create evil, because evil is not a substance.* Rather, evil is a *privation* or a *lack.* Evil is not a positive substance that God made—like a tree, a dog, or a human. It's not as though God made mountains and planets and lions and a clump of dark, swilling stuff called evil. *Rather, evil is just the absence of good where good should be.* Evil is like coldness (which is the absence of heat). Evil is like a shadow (which is the absence of light). Evil is like a hole in a shirt where shirt should be. The hole is not a substantial "thing." Rather, it is merely the absence of the cloth out of which the shirt is made; it is an absence of shirt where there should be shirt. In this defense, God created only things that are good, and therefore he is not evil. Evil is what we call it when someone takes a good thing that God has made and turns away from it. Evil is where one twists something good and uses it in a bad way (whether it be a will, an emotion, an action, or anything else). As another ancient theologian, St. Bonaventure, would say:

> *Sin is not any kind of essence but a defect and corruption . . . because the creature [humans] . . . may thus do something which is not from God, according to God, or because of God. This is sin, which is the corruption of mode, species, and order. Because sin is a defect, it cannot be said to have an efficient cause [i.e., something*

*that directly acts upon it to make it do something]; rather, it has a
deficient cause—namely, the defection of the created will.*[29]

What do you think of the arguments so far? Which ones are more
persuasive than others? Are none of them persuasive? Do you believe in
God (or gods), and if so, how do you deal with the problem of evil? If you
don't believe in God, then is evil even a real category and what does it mean?

Faith and reason

It is not an oversimplification to say that most of the philosophy done in
the Middle Ages was an attempt to understand how faith and reason go
together. Essentially, there are three ways to address this issue. The first is
to state that faith and reason are opposed and all we really need is faith. The
early church leader Tertullian is famous for asking, "What indeed has Athens to do with Jerusalem? What concord is there between the Academy and
the Church?" For Tertullian, what we need is faith, not reason. Whether or
not we can defend what we believe, or whether or not our arguments sound
ridiculous, is not a concern.

The Danish philosopher Søren Kierkegaard would also say that true
faith is not wedded to logic and reason. After all (to use an example Kierkegaard used), when God asked Abraham to sacrifice Isaac, there is no way that
Abraham could find that command reasonable. How could God command
Abraham to murder the promised child (through whom Abraham would
have descendants) when God was the one who had miraculously given him
Isaac to perpetuate his lineage in the first place? *For Kierkegaard, faith is a
"leap" away from reason.* Anytime someone thinks that faith is not really
"faith" if it is based on reason (or that reason and faith are opposites), they
are unknowingly submitting to Kierkegaard.

A second way to address this issue is to say that faith and reason are
opposed, and all we need is reason. This is certainly the view that comes out
in the Enlightenment and the view of philosophers who consider themselves
nonreligious. In this worldview, questions of faith are merely a hindrance to
true learning. Religion is a collection of superstitions passed down over the
generations. Our only hope is to allow reason to disprove, correct, and free
ourselves from the shackles of faith.

To what degree we unknowingly take nonreligious knowledge on faith
is sometimes overlooked by those who hold this position. Most of what we
know we don't know with certainty. Therefore, though it may not be religious faith, we all must use faith to some degree. We all hold positions that

are not based solely on what we can prove. But this is a different use of the word *faith* than how we are using it in this section on religion.

The third way to address this issue is the place where most of the medievals landed. *Faith and reason are both valid ways of finding truth; they just have different spheres of inquiry.* For the medieval philosophers, all truth is God's truth. They would say that there are some things that must be revealed to mankind that we cannot discover through reason (theological doctrines such as the Trinity). But there are other things that we can use reason to discover (like the existence of God). Most of the religious philosophy done in Europe throughout church history took this approach. This is why figures like Augustine combine Christianity with the philosophy of Plotinus and figures like Thomas Aquinas combine Christianity with the philosophy of Aristotle. As Aquinas would say:

> *The study of philosophy is legitimate and praiseworthy in itself. . . If, however, in the writings of the philosophers one finds anything contrary to faith, it is not philosophy but rather an abuse of philosophy stemming from a defect of reason. . . . Those who use philosophical texts in sacred teaching by subjugating them to faith, do not mix water with wine, but turn water into wine.*[30]

In this system, anything that is true belongs to God. So whether it comes from the field of philosophy, science, medicine, technology (or any other field), if it is a correct assessment of the world, then the religious believer is free to use it. However, they may use it only up to the point where it contradicts faith. Revelation (such as a sacred text) is held higher than reason, but reason is the "handmaid" that helps us understand it.

In the study of philosophy of religion, how do you think that faith and reason go together? Or, do they not go together? Which is primary? How do you know? Could there be knowledge that is beyond the limited scope of human reason? If so, how would we encounter it? If not, why? Is faith a hindrance to reason, or does reason help enlighten one's faith? Why?

Miscellaneous issues

We admittedly cannot cover every area related to religion in one chapter of an already short book on philosophy. So, in closing, we will simply ask some questions that will hopefully produce healthy conversation and debate among religious believers and nonreligious people alike.

In the philosophy of religion we can ask many questions. We can ask questions about God himself: What kind of being is God (or the gods)? Is he personal? Is he an energy or force? Is he immanent (meaning, close to humanity)? Is he transcendent (far away and far beyond our conception of him)? Is he both? Does he interact with the world or merely plan out how everything will transpire from the beginning and then step aside (like a giant clockmaker)? Is he infinite and wholly other? If so, how does he interact with the world? Is he not wholly other? If so, then how do you keep the distinction between Creator and creation in tact? Is he merely a being in the universe, or is he Being itself—the ground and source of existence? Is there one God or many? If you are a monotheist, is God triune (as in Christianity), or is he unitarian (as in Islam)?

We can also ask questions about other aspects of religion: What role should experience play in religion? After all, if God exists, then being able to somehow experience his presence or workings in the world would be expected. On the other hand, every religion claims to have experiences of the divine. How do we know who is right? Is faith "blind," or is it based on evidence? How certain do you have to be of something before you will believe it? How is belief in the existence of God different than personally trusting God? In what way does morality play into religion? Is asceticism holy, or should one enjoy life's pleasures (and which pleasures should be forbidden)?

Conclusion

Philosophy of religion is an intense and enormous topic. After all, it deals with some of our biggest questions (Why are we here? Is there a God? What started everything?). Philosophy of religion is not theology. Theology is an attempt to systematize beliefs about God. Philosophy of religion is where we put religion itself through the grid of logic and rationality to see how the two interact with one another. Everything from God's existence to miracles to religious experiences is the domain of philosophy of religion. But, unlike the cleric, we address the issues by using tools that are open to all, such as reason, argument, and dialectic.

For the religious believer, philosophy is something that helps them see their faith more clearly. For the nonbeliever, religion is something that gets in the way of reason. Are reason and faith antithetical or harmonious?

A theologian we have already mentioned (John Calvin) believed that all of our most important knowledge is either knowledge of God or knowledge of self. Now that we have thought a little about God, it is time to turn our attention to the topic of self.

Self

———————————————

Advertising has us chasing cars and clothes, working jobs we hate so we can buy shit we don't need. We're the middle children of history, man. No purpose or place. We have no Great War. No Great Depression. Our great war is a spiritual war. Our great depression is our lives. We've all been raised on television to believe that one day we'd all be millionaires, and movie gods, and rock stars, but we won't. We're slowly learning that fact. And we're very, very pissed off.

—Tyler Durden, *Fight Club*

———————————————

WHO ARE YOU REALLY? Are you primarily a material being, as Democritus thought? Are you primarily a political being, as Aristotle thought? Are you primarily a religious being, as Augustine thought? Are you primarily a thinking being, as Descartes thought? Are you primarily a perceived being, as Berkeley thought? Are you primarily an experiencing being, as Kierkegaard thought? Are you primarily a socialized being, as Rousseau thought? Are you primarily a monadic being, as Leibniz thought? Are you primarily an economic being, as Marx thought? Are you primarily an actualizing being, as Nietzsche thought? Are you primarily a sexual being, as Freud thought? Are you primarily a practical being, as Pierce thought? Are you primarily a liberating being, as Jefferson thought?

Or maybe you are not primarily one being at all. Maybe you have many "selves" or even no self. Are you just part of some grand "whole," as both Spinoza and Hegel thought? Or do you have a real, definable self (outside of the rest of the universe)? Do you have many selves and, perhaps, prefer to live one way or another depending on whom you are around? Are you one way at work, one way at school, one way with friends, and one way online? Or maybe who you are is not preset. Maybe you make yourself into whom you want to be. Jean-Paul Sartre held that it is your free decisions and how you decide to react to what life throws at you that allow you to truly become a certain type of self. He famously (and complicatedly) said, "No matter what is made of one, one is always responsible for what one makes of what is made of one." It really just rolls off the tongue, doesn't it?

Of course, you may think, "I know what makes me 'me.' After all, I seem aware of myself and aware of my body." But it's a bit more complicated than that. There is a famous thought experiment called the "Ship of Theseus" that I will change from a ship to a car to make it more contemporary. Pretend that your dad gave you a cherry-red, 1969 Chevelle before he passed away. His final instructions before he died were to keep the car in good running condition. He called his car "Mad Max." Every time you refer to that car, you call it Mad Max as well. Over the years you begin to replace different parts of Mad Max. You replace the tires, you replace the spark plugs, and you paint it a different color. No problem so far. It is still dad's car; it is still "Mad Max." But, over time, you end up replacing literally every single part of the car with new car parts. The gas tank is brand new; the doors are brand new; every part of the engine is brand new. After thirty years of working on it, there is not a single piece of the car that was originally there when your dad gave it to you. Here is the million-dollar question: Is it still Mad Max? Is it still your dad's car? Or, because it is made of entirely and only new parts, is it a new car? How the heck can it still be the same car if it literally has none of the parts the original car had?

How is this example of a car (that had its parts replaced) relevant to thinking about ourselves? Simply put, we are like that car. You may not have known this, but every single one of your cells is replaced several times in your lifetime . . . every single one. You are literally made up of entirely different cells then when you were a baby. So, are you still you?

To press the issue more, imagine that a man, John, murders someone when he is eighteen. Twenty years go by before John is caught by the authorities. Do the authorities have a right to sentence thirty-eight-year-old John for the murder that eighteen-year-old John did? Remember, none of the same cells that made up John twenty years ago are around anymore. This John is, materially speaking, a *completely new person*. The finger that pulled the trigger on the gun that he used to murder his victim has died and he has a completely new finger. How can we sentence a man for murder who is not made up of any of the parts of the John from the past who actually committed the murder? This is an oft-quoted problem for those who are pure materialists (those who think that the only thing that exists is matter). If you are indeed just matter (and all your matter changes), then you are essentially a completely different person as time goes on. This has caused philosophers to wonder what it is that makes you "you" and what makes me "me."

Or consider this thought experiment. The year is 3056. Science and technology have progressed to unimagined heights. Two people, Susan and Barbara, are lying side by side in a medical lab. A doctor, in the interest of science, puts Susan's brain into Barbara's body, and he puts Barbara's brain into Susan's body. Who is whom? Is it your body that makes you "you"? Is it your brain that makes you "you"? If Susan were married to a man named Brian, would he be cheating on her if he had sex with Barbara's body (even though Susan's brain is in Barbara's body)? And we can make the thought experiment even more interesting (and contemporary): Imagine you switched the brains of a straight woman with a gay man. The woman's brain would now be in the man's body. Would this woman now be gay if she were still attracted to men because she was in a man's body? Would the man cease to be gay because, though he was attracted to men, he was now in a woman's body?

What makes you "you"?

Some have thought that what makes you "you" is your body. Surely our body has something to do with who we are. But how much of your body can change before you stop being you? If you lose your hair, you are still you. If you get sunburned, you are still you. If you lose an arm, you are still you. This might sound trivial until I ask a very relevant cultural question: Can you change your genitalia and become a new person with a new name, new identity, or new gender? Does your body determine your gender, and if so, can you change your body to become a new person? If your body does not determine your gender, then why would someone want surgery to change their body to fit in with their new identity? Not to mention that we have already run into the issue above about how your body changes cells over your lifetime.

Some, in reaction, have swung the pendulum the other way and said that your body is not at all what makes you "you." Others have said that there must be an immaterial part of you that is your true identity. There must be a soul or mind that, though it interacts with your body, is distinct from your body.

For someone who is religious, they may believe that their soul is the "real" them. Their body may go into the ground when they die, but their soul may go to an afterlife. But then what is the soul, and how does it interact with the body if it's not material? And how do you respond to people who do not believe in "souls"? Perhaps you are more than your body, but would you say that you are not your body *at all*? We inherently think that one is linked to their body. After all, if a woman's body is assaulted, most would not say it was just an assault on her body. *Rather, they would say you have assaulted her, as a person.*

If your soul is the real you (and your body is not), then why do people think that actions done with the body affect the soul? Most would say if you murder with your body, you (i.e., your inner self) has committed the action as well. Conversely, when you fast and pray with your body, your soul is supposedly influenced. And, if your soul is the only thing that makes you "you," what do you do in a worldview that believes in reincarnation? If you were a man named Mike and you were reincarnated as a man named Patel, are Mike and Patel really the same person (though literally nothing about them is the same except their supposed "self" that can be reincarnated)?

Others have said that it is your memories that make you "you." After all, you have thoughts and a body, and I have thoughts and a body. What makes me different from you? Answer: we have different memories and experiences. It would be hard for me to be Zach if I didn't know anything about where I was born, who my parents were, what I like and don't like, who my friends were growing up, or anything else. Perhaps our memories are what make us "us."

But that seems to run into issues as well. After all, someone can get amnesia. Let's return again to our friend, John, the murderer. Let's say John murders someone, and as he is driving away from the scene of the crime, he gets into a wreck and loses all his memories. First, would John still be John? Second, and more interestingly, why would we charge him with the crime? If amnesia John—let's call him "New John"—if New John literally didn't know that he ever murdered anyone, and New John would not at all hurt someone today, and New John is really nice and not predisposed to violence at all, why would we lock him up? Would we want to protect society from him? That can't be the reason to lock him up, because New John now wouldn't hurt a fly. Would it to be "teach him a lesson"? I'm not sure he would get the lesson, because New John doesn't remember murdering the person. You're probably inclined to say we would lock him up, because it's still the same John who committed the murder. But here is where the rubber meets the road: *if memories are what makes you "you" and New John doesn't have any of the same memories as Old John, then you couldn't lock him up for murder because (by this definition) he would be a totally different person.*

Of course, there is also the skeptical answer that there is nothing that makes me "me." For some philosophers, there is no "me." For some philosophers, I happen to have a body and memories and such, but because all these things change, and because I don't have an immaterial soul or mind, then there is nothing that makes me "me." In this view there is no essential self. I just happen to be a clump of matter (a brain) inside a clump of matter (a body), and I have experiences. I am just clusters of experience but don't possess an actual me.

The mind-body problem

We all have trouble shaking the powerful suspicion that there is an internal self—an internal me. It seems as though there is a real me inside my body. I have consciousness, memories, and experiences. But this assumes that I am more than just my body. How does the immaterial part of me (if that even exists) and the material part of me go together?

Here we must discuss the fascinating issue of what is called the *mind-body problem* that has baffled philosophers ever since Descartes (and technically before him, to varying degrees).

In philosophy the "mind" is not the same thing as the "brain." The mind is the immaterial part of you that does the thinking. The brain is merely the material part of you—the grey matter in your head. Though many of us may think they are the same thing (which they may indeed be), I'll ask you to temporarily suspend that presupposition (and all its attendant implications) so you can really understand why this is a difficult issue.

Your mind is not the same thing as your brain. From a religious perspective, God (and angels) do not have brains, but they still think. Additionally (also from a religious perspective), if you have a soul, then after you die, though your brain is buried in the ground, your soul (the mind or thinking part of you) would then live on (in heaven; hell; the river Styx; Orlando, Florida; or wherever souls go).

From a nonreligious perspective, the mind still seems to be different from the brain for the simple reason that the material lump of gray matter is not the same as the subjective, conscious experience that I have. Let's perform a thought experiment to elucidate how one's thoughts and conscious experiences are different than that wrinkly, raisin-looking organ we call a brain: Think of a pink elephant. In your mind you are able to picture that large Dumbo-looking creature and color it pink. That is your thought of the elephant. *Notice that your thought of the pink elephant is completely different than the chemicals and neurons that fire in your brain to think of the elephant.* If your conscious experience of the pink elephant were material, then I should be able to cut into your skull and find a pink elephant somewhere in the brain. After all, if your thought experience is made of matter, I should be able to see something made of matter. However, if I were to surgically open your head, I would find electrical impulses and chemicals, *but I would not find a tiny pink elephant anywhere (though you are thinking of one).* Nothing going on in your brain processes looks anything like the image of the pink elephant. If the thought of the pink elephant was material or if the mind was only material, then we should expect to find a tiny pink elephant somewhere in your head when we performed brain surgery. The pink elephant is actually immaterial, because it is thought by your mind, which may not be identical to the material processes in the brain. *Isn't that absolutely amazing?*

Our thoughts seem to be made of something that is not material. When I think of a pink elephant, that image and the subjective experience I have while thinking about it are completely different than the material and physical processes going on in my brain. If I thought about a pink elephant while my brain was connected to a computer, we would be able to see certain parts of the brain "light up." We would see electrical signals firing, and we would see chemicals changing, but the actual thought itself would not show up on the screen—a pink elephant would not appear on the medical screen. It seems as though our thoughts, though they actually exist, are not made of matter but something more.

An MRI of the brain gives a complete look at everything physical. A doctor can see if you have a tumor, for example, only because the MRI sees every contour of your physical brain. And yet, the person having the MRI is thinking several thoughts while the scan is happening. Perhaps they are thinking about vacation. Perhaps they are thinking about their spouse. Perhaps they are thinking about a pink elephant. If their thoughts (and mind) were physical, then the technician or doctor conducting the MRI should be seeing physical images of a vacation, their spouse, and a pink elephant on the screen in the exact same way that they can see a brain tumor. The fact that the MRI doesn't see any of these ideas causes us to ask if thoughts (and the mind) are physical.

Don't get me wrong, our brain seems to somehow interact with what philosophers call our "mind" when we think, but the actual image that we create is not identical to any material process in the brain. I can imagine the concept of infinity without needing an infinite number of brain cells to do it.

I can think of pink elephants that, even if you connect my brain up to electrodes, do not show the same image of a pink elephant on the screen (but rather just show wavelengths). In this sense, reading someone's thoughts is impossible. Yes, we could teach a computer that some x electrical signal equals some y thought and program the computer to try to draw a picture of what someone was thinking, *but that would allow the computer only to follow a program we taught it; it would not allow anyone to actually see our thoughts exactly like we do.*

This is why the concept of a lie detector test is misguided. A polygraph (or lie detector) test cannot measure truth at all. *It also cannot measure your thoughts at all.* All it can measure is bodily responses like heart rate and blood pressure. If you ask an atheist who is connected to a polygraph if God exists, he will say no. If you ask a theist if God exists, he will say yes. The lie detector test will say they are both telling the truth. But that can't be the case, because they are saying opposite (and contradictory) things. *What the polygraph test is doing is measuring bodily responses that vary depending on whether or not the person speaking* believes *they are telling the truth.* But a calm liar and a nervous truth teller would give the test false readings. The polygraph is a material device that can read only biological changes; it cannot truly get into the person's immaterial thoughts to know what they are thinking. This is one of the reasons why polygraph tests are no longer admissible in court.

Now that we have laid out the possibility that your thoughts (and mind) may be different than your brain processes (and cerebral cortex), it is time to ask the deep questions. If they are different substances, how do they interact? How can my thoughts move my body? How can my body cause me to have different thoughts? How does the mind (which is a different substance than the body) interact with the body?

This is another aspect of the famous mind-body problem. If I were to stare at the water bottle on my desk and, through just my mental willpower, cause it to float, that would be absolutely amazing. *But the fact that, through just my mental willpower, I can raise my hand when I will to do so (by using immaterial thoughts) is just as amazing.* I'm literally using my immaterial thoughts in my immaterial mind to move my material arm. But how does that happen? How does the idea jump the gap from being my thought or my will (which, as we've seen with the pink elephant example, is not physical) to being able to move my physical arm?

If you are a bit confused, let's use another example. Is pain or emotion the exact same thing as the chemical processes in the brain that cause emotion? When I feel pain in my toe, the pain itself is actually something different than the chemical reaction in my brain. The reaction in my brain is causing me to think that there is pain in my toe. But what's crazy is that the chemical reaction is going on in my head and is nowhere near my toe. *The chemical impulses that I interpret as pain are different than the pain itself.* But if that is the case, how do they interact?

Or consider the emotion sadness. Is the experienced emotion the exact same thing as chemical processes that cause sadness? Yes, it's true that people who are depressed can have varying levels of hormones and neurological deficiencies that cause them to be sad. But that seems different from the feeling of sadness that the person actually experiences. A person who has been dead for only one second would have a very similar brain chemistry as the person just before they died, but they wouldn't be sad. The person who has been dead for only one second would still have the same stimulus causing the pain in their toe as they had when they were alive, but they wouldn't have pain. If the mind is the same thing as the brain, then why does there seem to be such a large difference between actual pain or sadness and the purely chemical brain processes that themselves are neither sad nor painful? To say it another way, chemicals cannot be sad or feel pain. Only people can be sad or feel pain—only *minds* can feel pain or be sad.

This is what led René Descartes to assert that animals didn't feel pain. That sounds crazy to us today, and regardless of what you think, you don't have a right to go home and kick your pet. What would lead him to say such a heartless thing? Surely animals feel pain, right? For Descartes, we as humans are primarily thinking things (a mind or soul) and we have a physical body. But an animal doesn't have a rational, moral mind. They are, therefore, not a "self" and are more like a fleshy machine. Sure, your puppy looks sad, but that doesn't mean he actually feels sadness. Sure, your puppy looks like he is guilty when he poops on the floor, but since he doesn't have a soul, he can't actually feel guilt. If your dog had a mind or soul, instead of "all dogs go to heaven," he might be judged by God to go to puppy hell for being a bad dog. Sure, your puppy yelps when you accidentally step on his foot, but that doesn't mean he feels pain. When you think that your puppy experiences pain, what you are doing, according to Descartes, is *reading your experience of pain back onto the puppy.* When someone steps on your foot, because you are a rational agent with consciousness, you have a "self" that feels pain. You then read that experience onto the puppy and assume they have a mind (like yours) as well. But you don't ever actually know that they have a mind. All you see is the puppy react to external stimuli.

Let's say that I made a robotic puppy that had all the same processes as a biological puppy. I program it to give you big, sad, puppy eyes when you do something that produces "sorrow." I program it to look guilty after it drops mechanical dog poop pellets on the carpet. I even program it to yelp and run away when you step on its foot. After a while, you might start to believe that the dog actually feels sadness, guilt, or pain. However, the robot dog feels nothing, because it doesn't have a mind/soul. It merely follows computer procedures in each of these processes. How do you know that a real, biological dog isn't doing the exact same thing? How do you know the fact that the dog yelps when you step on its foot isn't just like the robot dog—that the dog is biologically programmed to yelp and run away to preserve its life, though it doesn't actually feel the pain in a little doggy soul or "self"? You see, when we discuss the issue of what makes you "you," the mind-body problem continues to disorient us from every side. We want to say the real me is something internal to me, but when we define that as something other than the body (and other than matter), we run into some tricky issues. If you don't have a self, then a dog doesn't have a self either.

One more example before moving on: Imagine someone who has phantom limb syndrome. This is where someone who has lost a limb still feels like they have one. Many amputees report still feeling as though their missing limb is still there. They might feel as though their hand is itching, even though they don't have a hand. They might feel pain in their arm, even though they don't have an arm. This is a strange phenomenon indeed. But it is also helpful in explaining the mind-body problem. *Notice that the pain that the person feels in their arm can't be the same as when they had an arm.* First, they don't have an arm, so their arm can't be telling them they are in pain. What then is telling them they are in pain? You might say their brain is telling them they are in pain. But how does that work? The brain is telling them there is pain in a limb they don't have, which means the pain is not really there. But the person certainly feels like it is there. Some patients report extreme pain in the limb that they have lost.

An arm that isn't there can't feel pain. Also, chemicals can't feel pain. The brain changes chemicals and electrical impulses to tell the amputee that they have pain in their arm, but the chemicals themselves are not painful. If they were, then the patient would feel pain in their head (where the chemicals were changing) and not in their arm (which they no longer have). It seems as though the subjective conscious experience of pain is quite different than the chemicals that supposedly cause it.

How do we solve this conundrum? How is it that things such as thoughts, feelings, imagination, willpower, mind, and our experienced (subjective) experience all seem to be immaterial, but they are able to interact with cells, ligaments, blood vessels, and muscles? How can our thoughts move our bodies? How can our bodies affect our thoughts?

Are the mind and the brain identical?

You may, of course, be tempted to say that, to avoid the mind-body problem, the mind is the exact same thing as the brain. That would solve the problem of how they can interact. A material brain could move a material body, and a material body could affect a material brain. But this "solution" opens up a whole host of other problems. For example, as we saw earlier, this would mean that you have absolutely no free will. If your mind is just your material brain, then you are like a computer. Impulses go in, and impulses go out. Whatever physically happens to you necessarily causes you to react the way you do. But this means that the person who murdered someone *had* to murder them. They were simply doing what their mechanical brain was hardwired to do, based on impulses it received from a causal chain of their physical surroundings. This we have briefly discussed earlier in the book. But something we haven't discussed yet is that, if your mind is just your material brain, then you would not feel any love, or sadness, or bravery.

For example, would you consider a robot brave just because it ran out into battle (without hesitation) and was instantly blown up? The answer is no. Because a robot is constituted solely of matter, it cannot be brave, because it has no fear that it has to overcome (which is what bravery is—the overcoming of fear). It simply does as it is programmed. If the mind and the brain are the same, then this means that no human has ever acted bravely. Stimulus went into their brain, which caused them to run out into battle, thus allowing them to be blown up. At no point did they make a conscious "choice" to do something daring. To have a real choice, you have to have a will, but if the brain and the mind are the same, then you don't have a will. Perhaps humans are not just biological computers or robots. Perhaps the issue is trickier than many scientists make it seem.

This leads to the interesting question of artificial intelligence. If the brain is the same thing as the mind, then perhaps humans are like robots or robots are like humans. Could a robot really ever "think" on its own? Obviously, we can use a program to teach a computer to "learn." But what do we mean by "learn"? The computer, by "learning" new information is only following a program that we created (which told it how to acquire more information on its own). But here is the kicker: *the computer never consciously and self-reflectively knows that's what it is doing.* It acquires new information (and that is what we think of as artificial intelligence), but only because our initial program allowed it to accomplish this task. It doesn't have a real mind. Could we ever make a computer so sophisticated that it actually could feel pain or love? Would we really send a robot to jail for murdering someone so it could be punished for its crime? That would be stupid. A robot isn't afraid of jail or dying because it was never alive. It's just wires and metal.

According to philosopher John Searle, humans and robots are not the same, *and robots will never truly be intelligent.* Humans have self-reflective consciousness that a robot will never have. Artificial intelligence, in the *true* sense of the term, can't really exist. Searle gives a famous example known as the Chinese Room (which I will heavily modify for clarity).[31]

Imagine that you don't know a lick of Mandarin, and you, as an English speaker, are locked in a large room in China. There is a guard who stands outside your door, but he never speaks. To get your food allotment for the day, a guard will slide you a Chinese symbol under the door, written on a piece of paper, and you have to slide him back a different Chinese symbol. You have to take the symbol he sent you, look at it, and then hand him back a different Chinese symbol, or you will not receive your food. How do you know which symbol to hand back to him? On the wall there is a large code—a large cypher—that simply shows which symbol you should hand the guard depending on which symbol he first hands you. With me so far?

So, the guard hands you a Chinese letter that looks like a squiggly line. You look up at the code on the wall and it shows you that if you get a Chinese letter with a squiggly line, then you should pass back a symbol that has a circle. The next day the guard slides you a Chinese symbol that looks like a jagged line. You look up at the chart on the wall and it shows that if you get a symbol with a jagged line, you should hand back a symbol that looks like a small tree. The next day the guard hands you a symbol that looks like a tornado, so you look at the wall and hand him back the corresponding symbol that looks like three lines. Each day you get a different symbol, and each day you slide back the corresponding symbol so you can get your food.

Here is the point of the experiment: Does handing back a symbol (you don't understand) in response to a symbol you received (that you don't understand) ever allow you to actually learn Chinese? *The answer is a resounding no.* Remember, you also are never told what any of the Chinese symbols mean. You literally get an input and give an output. You even get new inputs and send out new outputs. But you never acquire the ability to speak fluent Mandarin. You never really grow in your intelligence of the actual language of Mandarin. But someone who was watching you from the outside (the same way we watch "intelligent" robots) would think that you were indeed someone who speaks Chinese. They would see how quickly you look at a symbol and then pass back a corresponding symbol and jump to the conclusion that you understand the meaning of all the symbols. It would look like you were having a conversation with the guard, but you wouldn't be having a conversation at all. You would just be following the rules of the chart on the wall, even though you didn't have a clue what any of the symbols mean.

What Searle is doing is showing that a computer is just like the example of the Chinese room. We slide the computer an input and it gives us a preprogrammed output. We give it a symbol and it gives us the corresponding symbol from the very chart, or cypher, that we gave it originally. Searle's argument shows that robots, no matter how much we think they "understand," *can't truly understand.* Searle's argument is interesting, especially when some philosophers today try to play it in reverse. If it is the case that robots cannot truly understand, does this mean that humans are more than biological robots? Does the fact that we have understanding mean that some part of us is immaterial? Or, is our mind actually material (just our brain) and we simply don't know how it interacts with our body?

What do you think so far? If your thoughts are physical, then why can't we find a tiny, material pink elephant in your head when you think of one? If your mind is immaterial, then how can it interact with material objects?

The philosophical problem with psychology

Most people have never thought about how psychology is directly linked to the issues of self and the mind-body problem. When we think of psychology, we typically just think of someone holding a notepad counseling someone else who is lying on a couch by saying things like "Tell me about your childhood" or "When did you first start having this dream?" However, it may be shocking to know that psychology is a relatively new field of study and has often had to seek to justify itself as a true science. For most of Western history, it was merely a subset of philosophy. That sounds strange to those of us who live after Freud. What could be more scientific than psychology? But the reason it has often taken so much heat from the older sciences (what are called the "hard sciences," such as physics and biology) is due again to the issue Descartes bequeathed to us in the mind-body problem.

Psychology is technically the study of the soul (the Greek word *psuchē* means "soul" or "inner life"). This leads one to ask, "If psychology is the study of the soul, then what exactly does it study?" How do you study the "soul"? You may be tempted to say that the psychologist studies something material, like the brain. But that's not psychology; that is neurology (brain science). So that answer won't do. After all, psychologists cannot perform brain surgery. In contrast, you might say the psychologist is studying something that is not material—the "mind" or the "soul." But that's not psychology; that is religion. *If psychology studies something material, like the brain, then it ceases to be psychology and simply becomes neurology. If psychology studies something immaterial, like the mind, inner life, or soul, it ceases to be psychology and becomes religion.* So . . . does it study something material or immaterial?

What exactly is it studying? If it is studying the inner life (mind), then we have to assume that there is a mind/soul that is not material and science goes out the window. But if we think that it is studying a part of the body (brain), then we should be dealing only with medical doctors and not counselors. The psychologist is stuck playing the role of either the cognitive scientist or the priest, but to a lesser degree than either. Perhaps, as B. F. Skinner thought, the role of psychology is simply to study behavior. After all, maybe humans are big machines and the goal is simply to get them to act differently, regardless of their internal state. *How are we supposed to help people if we are not even sure what their inner life is?* Why should we go to counselors or psychologists if we can't even put our finger on *exactly* what they study?

The American father of psychology, William James, made fun of Freud for his views of the subconscious and psychoanalysis for the very fact that we can't consciously understand what, by definition, cannot be made conscious. He said that Freud's method was "the sovereign means for believing what one likes in psychology, and of turning what might become a science into a tumbling-ground for whimsies."[32] James points out something we saw when we discussed Karl Popper. For something to truly be science, there must be a way to disprove it. Much that is done under the name of science in the field of psychology fails to meet Popper's falsification principle. James mocks Freud, because one can say whatever they like and call it "psychology." Someone can be depressed because they are around too many or too few people. Someone can be anxious because they have too little or too much control of their life. Someone can leave their spouse because of their childhood trauma or become codependent on their spouse because of their childhood trauma. It is very difficult for counselors to pretend that their field of study is held to the same level of falsification and scrutiny as, say, a neurologist or brain surgeon.

What is the ultimate goal of the counselor? Is it to get you to act a different way (the job of the behavioralist or ethicist)? Is it to assess you spiritually (the job of the pastor)? Is it to cure chemical imbalances in your brain (the job of the medical doctor)? Is it to make you feel better (the job of the motivational speaker or drug dealer)? Is it to help you understand something from your past (the job of the historian)?

To be crystal clear: none of this is to downplay the helpful and beneficial insights from psychology. I think studying psychology is fascinating, *and I know many people who have been helped by the work of psychologists.* But, as we saw in the chapter on science, just because something works (and has positive, practical effects) doesn't mean that it is *true knowledge.* Psychology shows us how difficult it is to understand what it is that makes me "me," and it shows us how the mind-body problem plays into areas of life that are not just the realm of the philosopher. As James pointed out, we must ask the person trying to help us in our "inner life" if they are there to help us with something that is not scientific (such as our immaterial mind/soul) or something that is scientific (such as our brain chemistry or synapses). The counselor who cannot answer that question should, perhaps, not be in that field of inquiry.

Conclusion

We have seen how difficult it is to ask the question "What makes me 'me'?" Perhaps there is nothing that makes me "me." Perhaps there is no self. Perhaps I have many selves. Perhaps I have a most true self. What do we mean when we say "I don't feel like myself"? How could one not feel like what they are?

We have also seen how difficult it is to answer the question of how the parts of us that don't seem material (such as our subjective, conscience experiences) affect the bodily and material parts of us. Perhaps we are only matter. Perhaps we are more than only matter. No matter (pun) what answer you give, you run into problems.

So far, this chapter has been a bit individualistic. Most of it has caused us to look at just ourselves as individual beings. Do community and the people we are around contribute to our self? After all, no man is an island (which is true metaphorically and metaphysically). In what ways do we function and find meaning in larger society? The topic of self combines with this issue as we approach our next chapter: justice.

Justice

WHAT IS JUSTICE? Everyone seems to long for it. Every political system, from Pharaoh's Egypt, to Charlemagne's Europe, to Stalin's USSR, to Hitler's Germany claims to be "just." But what is it for a society to be just, and how should we understand justice? This chapter will deal with the issue of political philosophy and how justice and society can be defined in relation to one another.

Today, we take for granted our current political system. In most Western nations, we assume that citizens should all have the right to vote. We assume that the leaders should rule at the consent of the governed. We assume that we have natural rights. We assume that there should be checks and balances. We assume that the law applies to every person equally. But, and this may shock you, this was not always the case.

For someone like Plato, a just society would include:

> *Members of the upper classes are not allowed to marry; women*
> *are to be held in common and all sexual intercourse is to be public.*
> *Procreation is the be strictly regulated on eugenic grounds. Chil-*
> *dren are not to be allowed contact with their parents, but will be*
> *brought up in public creches. Guardians and auxiliaries may not*
> *own property or touch money; they will be given, free of charge,*
> *adequate but modest provisions, and they will live in common like*
> *soldiers in a camp.*[33]

This is a very different world than what we expect today. Consider how different our society is from the Ming Dynasty, the theocracy of ancient Israel, or Sharia law in Saudi Arabia. Consider what it would be like to fight for your life in the Colosseum after committing a crime or to be on trial for heresy during the Salem witch trials. One doesn't have to go very far back in history to see that social and political life was very different for most of world history than it is today. Even if you say that ancient Greece had a similar political structure because they "invented democracy," it would be wise to remember that their democracy also accepted slavery, allowed only free males to vote, and would vote to go to war if a seer believed the gods had commanded it.

Questioning our presuppositions

It is very hard for most Westerners to truly believe that the past is a foreign place. We assume that everyone has always thought the same way that we do. In studying justice and political philosophy, we have to lay our assumptions aside and try to honestly consider varying views, even if they seem crazy. For example, it is a staple of modern, Western nations to have some form of democracy. We cannot imagine a world where people don't have the right to select their leaders. Democracy is certainly a cornerstone of industrialized nations.

But, for most of Western history (and especially for our good friend Plato), rule by democracy was an absurd idea. After all, why would we want mob rule? If the masses can be ignorant and selfish, why on earth would we want them deciding the laws for an entire country? The problem with democracy for many ancient writers is that *it counts heads instead of weighing arguments.* Do we really want all people having the same political power? Why would we allow someone who thinks the world is flat to have the same say in government as someone with a PhD in public policy from Harvard? Why should someone who owns no property in a country have as much say in what happens as someone who owns large tracts of land (since the governmental decisions affect the person with more land to a much higher degree than the person who is not a property owner)? Do people usually vote for what is best for everyone equally, or conversely, do they vote in a selfish way for whatever will most benefit them, their pet projects, or their identity groups?

This is not to throw democracy under the bus. After all, as Winston Churchill once quipped, "Democracy is the worst form of government except for all those other forms that have been tried." It is simply to try to get you to question your presuppositions—*even the presuppositions that you hold most dearly*. Political philosophy is similar to ethics in that it comes with a lot of emotional baggage. You may argue empiricism versus rationalism until you are blue in the face, but most people don't assassinate governmental leaders over an issue of epistemology. Politics, however, motivates people to action. Political thought strikes at the heart of some of our deepest and most important beliefs. *Because of this, most people don't ever change their political stance.* When challenged, they just dig their heels in deeper. For this chapter, however, I'll ask you not to do that. Please give different views a chance and doubt your own view (whether left, right, or center) as much (or more!) than you doubt the views of others. Until you're really able to apologize for previous beliefs and change your mind when good evidence is presented, you'll never be a philosopher.

In discussing justice, we are not going to be doing political science. We are not interested in looking at individual, particular cases of political action in our twenty-first-century, limited context. Because of this, we are not looking at individual political issues that most Americans care about today (gun control, global warming, policing, immigration, tort reform, etc.). We are also not addressing economics. Economics certainly has its place, but it is not the same type of inquiry as political philosophy. Rather, as philosophers, our job is to analyze the questions behind the assumptions of both political science and economics. Our job is not to say "How does our government work today?" or "How is the economy doing under the new president?" Rather, we have weightier (and more foundational) questions like "How *should* governments function?" "What are 'rights' and how do we apply them equally?" and "What form of government leads to the highest level of human flourishing?" Until we have a good political philosophy in place, we will find ourselves building political castles in the sand. We must have a solid ideological foundation on which we can then apply the practical implementation of politics. This is the goal of studying justice.

You might wonder why we are discussing politics at all. After all, isn't this supposed to be a book on philosophy? Well, it turns out that all political views stand on philosophical foundations. Without uncovering these foundations, we won't ever be able to create a better system of justice. Let's use America's two-party system as an example of assumed underlying foundations.

In the US, though there are various political parties, the only two that ever gain any traction are the Democratic and Republican parties. Think about all the differences between these two. First, they have different colors associated with them. Republicans are red, and Democrats are blue. But these were not the original colors of the right and the left. The original color of the right was white (which had nothing to do with race), and the original color of the left was actually red (which is why Communist nations such as China, North Korea, and the former USSR used the color red). The terms *right* and *left* came from parliamentary seating locations during the time of the French Revolution. But terms and colors are not the main focus of each group.

Those on the left believe that we should look to the *future* for definitions of justice, truth, and goodness. This is why they are also called "progressives." They have an ideal toward which they want to *progress* (instead of looking to how things were done in the past). They lean toward a pure democracy, a regulated market, positive rights, communitarianism, and have a tendency to ask "What would be ideal?"

Those on the right believe we should look to the past for definitions of justice, truth, and goodness. This is why they are also called "conservatives." They have an ideal that they want to maintain (i.e., conserve) from previous generations (instead of changing certain foundations as we move toward the future). They lean toward limits on mass rule, a deregulated market, negative rights, individualism, and have a tendency to ask "What would practically work?"

You might not have caught this yet, but look how chock-full of philosophy these two positions are! For example, when there is a mass shooting in a school, those on the left will blame easy access to guns, and those on the right will blame the character of the person who did the shooting. This isn't just about public policy; *it is a philosophical debate on whether or not human nature is intrinsically good (like Rousseau taught) or intrinsically bad (like Hobbes taught).* If you think humans are basically good, then you want a larger government to help people. If you think humans are basically bad, then you want a smaller government to prevent tyranny.

Or consider the question, "What is marriage?" For someone on the left, the definition of things lies in the future—marriage can change meaning as society changes. For someone on the right, the definition lies in the past—marriage means what it has meant for most of Western history. *Notice how deeply philosophical this so-called political issue actually is.* Do we look to the past to find things that are true, or do we shape truth by what we do as we strive toward the future? How old is truth, goodness, or beauty? Are these old ideas to be retained or new ideas to be reimagined?

There is no doing politics without having one's philosophical presuppositions silently scream for attention behind each issue. This is also why it is so hard to change someone's mind on political issues. Everyone tries to talk about the issues: immigration, the wage gap, green energy, etc., without ever stopping and doing philosophy. You can't ask "What should we do about immigration?" until you have asked the better question of "What role does a government owe to noncitizens?" If we were clearer about the worldview we held before discussing politics, we would have more fruitful conversations and less division.

In studying justice, we will look at a smattering of topics, but perhaps we will begin with the concept of equality. After all, justice is, at least tangentially, linked to the concept of equality. But what is equality?

Equality

Is equality always a good thing? To even ask the question sounds crazy, because it seems to have an obvious answer. "Yes, of course it is always good to have equality," we want to say.

But is that true? Is every *type* of equality good? Should everyone be the same height? Should everyone have the same sexual rights to another person's spouse? Should everyone be required to wear the same clothing? Should everyone have the same right to perform surgery, with or without a medical license? Should everyone be the same weight? Should everyone get paid the same amount even when the difficulty of their jobs varies significantly? Should everyone be equally allowed to work in a daycare, regardless of their criminal record?

And what do we do with people who are more talented than others? To make everyone equal (in all ways), should we make smart people less intelligent? Should we injure exceptionally athletic people? Should we deface and scar the bodies of those who are more beautiful than others so they become equal to others in beauty? To make everyone equal in every way includes taking those who are exceptional and making them mediocre.

The more closely we examine the concept of equality, the more clearly we see that, if we really care about justice, we will need some nuance. *Some types of equality are good, and some types of equality are bad.* Equality is a neutral term that can be used in either positive or negative ways. Some types of equality are good. It is good for people of varying races to be allowed to vote and to have their vote counted equally. It is good for both men and women to be allowed to testify in court. It is good to protect the constitutional rights of the poor. But some types of a false, so-called equality are bad. It is bad to take someone's inheritance and give it to others. It is bad to allow someone sexual access to another person's spouse against their consent. *It is essential that we do not embrace all forms of equality or else we will find out that we are creating actual inequalities.*

How can this be? How can an attempt at equality promote inequality? How can we know what we mean by the term *equality* and whether it is being used in a way that is truly just or as a sleight-of-hand to promote some political agenda? In discussing equality, it is helpful to distinguish formal equality from material equality. *Formal equality* is equality before the law. It is constitutional equality. Formal equality allows someone to pursue their own ends and not be excluded based on factors such as the color of their skin or their religion. Formal equality means that legal barriers cannot be put up to keep you from seeking after your goals. In formal equality, people have equality of legal opportunity. Some may have to work harder than others to achieve the same goals (because we all start from different places), but if one is willing to put in the sweat equity, then one can achieve something great. Formal equality is equality de jure.

But there is a very different type of equality that looks for not equality of legal opportunity but equality of outcome—equality of result. It is called *material equality.* In material equality, what matters is whether or not you have the same *outcome* as another person. The most extreme form of material equality is communism (which is why Marx defined it in the *Communist Manifesto* as the "abolition of private property"). But one certainly doesn't have to go that far on the spectrum to support some level of material equality. Whereas formal equality is equality de jure, material equality is equality de facto. Formal equality is in principle; material equality is in outcome.

One should note that these two views of equality are contradictory. If you think everyone should have formal equality, then this necessarily leads to material inequality. If everyone has equality in the sense of the same standing before the law (which is already the case in countries like the US), then this means that people will not have the same "stuff" at the end of the day. People who use money wisely will have very different lives from people who invest money poorly. Conversely, if a society has material equality, then one cannot have formal equality. If a wealthy person's money is taken and given to the disenfranchised (so they have an equal outcome), then they are not being treated equally in principle. One person is having a rule apply to them that does not apply to another person.

Which one of these forms of equality do you believe is correct? Which form do you prefer? Which form does the US Constitution defend? Is the Constitution correct on this issue?

Let's give a few examples of each type of equality. If a black person was applying to Harvard and they were not allowed to attend because of their skin color, that would certainly be inequality. That would be denying the student formal equality, because regardless of how smart they were or how hard they worked, they would not be allowed to pursue their own ends because of their race. This would be a true injustice. Now imagine that Harvard says that, to avoid inequality, they must hire the same number of black professors as white professors. Is that formal or material equality? That is material equality. In that second scenario, they are defining equality by the end result and not by the standard of equal opportunity. At the writing of this chapter, about 13% of the US population is black; Harvard, in this example, is saying that their institution is acting in a racist way unless 50% of their professors are black. Notice how different the definition of equality is when we talk about it in a formal sense versus a material sense.

To give another example, would it be wrong for an intelligent person in a wheelchair to denied access to a desk job for no other reason than the fact that they couldn't walk? Yes, that would indeed be wrong. But is it inequality if most of the business's employees are able-bodied? No, it is not. Again, we have to be very precise when we define equality. To deny someone in a wheelchair the right to a desk job for the sole reason that they cannot walk would be taking something that is not relevant to their performance (in this case, being disabled) and excluding them. But it is not a formal inequality to forbid someone in a wheelchair from being a police officer (who is required to chase criminals), for example, because the ability to run is extremely relevant to the job of being a police officer.

Or consider another scenario: A person claims they are being treated unequally because they can't get into Yale (due to the fact that they have neither the grades nor the money to attend). Is that actual inequality? Again, it is not. To not allow someone into a university because they are not as talented or cannot pay their bills is not denying them an equal right in formal equality; it is denying them only the (alternate) type of material equality. In this case, the student was not being denied some legal or constitutional right; rather, they were not financially or academically qualified to be allowed into the institution.

Note: If you haven't gotten mad and thrown the book across the room yet, you're doing well. You see? Emotion creeps into our hearts when we discuss political philosophy. Some of you are already upset by something I said in this chapter, and I haven't even made a case for any particular position. Some of you think that formal equality is the problem with the world and that people should have more equality of outcome. Some of you think that material equality is the problem with the world and the people should have the government stay out of their lives. Whichever side you fall on, please try to suspend your biases and really understand the other side—because this chapter is only going to get worse.

Constitutional equality, or fairness, is a good thing. Everyone should be treated the same before the law. For some philosophers, true equality is treating everyone the same. In this definition, no one gets any additional favors that others do not get. But others disagree. Others say that by treating everyone the same, you are not giving a leg up to those who need it the most. *They would claim that treating people unequally will lead to the most equality.* But again, the issue here is formal versus material equality. You cannot have both. You must choose which one is more just.

Lastly, in discussing equality, we should briefly discuss whether or not all *cultures* are equal. Most of us do (or should) agree that all *races* are equal. Racism has no part in a modern liberal democracy. But this is not at all the same question as asking if all *cultures* are equal. Races and cultures are not the same categories. China, Japan, and Laos are all Asian, but their cultures are very different. Spain, Brazil, and Mexico are all Hispanic, but their cultures are very different. Again, our gut reaction when asked "Are all cultures equal?" is to give a resounding "Yes!" But do you believe the culture of Nazi Germany in 1942 is equal to the culture of modern-day Belgium? Probably not. Or what about a culture that practices cannibalism? Is their culture as good and as free and as just as a culture that abhors cannibalism? In fact, as soon as someone says that all cultures are equal, the sassy philosopher can reply, "What about a culture that doesn't think all cultures are equal? Is that culture as equal as a culture that does think that all cultures are equal?" It is important when thinking about justice to separate culture from race. All people, regardless of race, deserve justice within a modern republic. But this does not mean that everyone's culture is equal in every respect (as some cultures even seek to destroy other cultures).

Equality is a difficult issue, and it is related to what it truly means to live in a free country. What does it mean to be free? How should we as philosophers think of freedom?

Freedom

What is freedom? What are rights? By *freedom*, in this section we are talking about political freedom. We are not discussing ontological freedom, which we dealt with earlier—the question about how we could have a free will if everything is causally determined by materialism (or by the sovereignty of a deity).

When discussing freedom we again have to define our terms and use nuance. Many people hide presuppositions behind the words *freedom, liberty,* and especially *rights.* What kind of rights do you really have? What does the government owe its citizens? When talking about freedom and rights, there are primarily two ways that we can think about them. The first is called negative rights (negative freedom). The second is called positive rights (positive freedom).

Freedom as defined in light of *negative rights* means that what the government owes you is the duty to get out of the way of your freedoms (and to prevent others from hindering your freedoms). The government's job, in this view, is not to provide positive things for you (such as medical care or an education). Rather, *their job is to make sure that they (and others) do not get in the way of you doing what you want to do.* You, as a citizen, get to decide how to live your life (assuming you're not breaking the law), and the government's job is to make sure that you are not arrested unfairly, that someone doesn't try to steal your property, or that someone doesn't try to limit your freedom to think and say what you want. You have the right to pursue your own interests, and others may not violate that right. It is "negative" because the government is not giving you additional things in life. Rather, *they are keeping things from infringing on your right to live life the way you see fit.* In this view, rights are things like freedom of speech, freedom of religion, freedom to not have to testify against yourself, the right to keep your private property, etc. This is the view of rights (rightly or wrongly) enshrined in the US Constitution—which doesn't guarantee life, liberty, and property (the last of these being a *positive* right)—but which guarantees life, liberty, and the pursuit of happiness (all *negative* rights).

There is, in contrast, another way that people talk about rights. This is the idea of *positive rights.* Someone who believes in positive rights asserts that the government doesn't just owe you a life where you can do what you want by keeping other people from infringing upon your liberties. Rather, they believe that the government *owes you positive goods.* Positive rights are things like healthcare, education, housing, and others. With negative rights, your life is yours for the taking; the government's job is to free you up. With positive rights, the government's job is to actively give you something. The proponent of positive rights will say that the right to life is not simply that you have a life but that you need certain things to enhance the *quality* of your life (which the government should provide for you). Why would the government simply get out of your way if they can also provide you with things that make your life better? For example, when people say that healthcare is a right, this is the notion of rights they have in mind. They are saying the government should give you the positive benefit of medical care.

Which of these views of rights is correct, and why? What are the problems if the government provides only negative rights? How will the property rights (especially money) of other people be infringed upon if we give people positive rights (after all, the money to give everyone education, for example, must come from somewhere)? Conversely, how can people exercise their right to pursue happiness if they start off farther behind the starting line than other people? Most importantly for the philosopher: What does a government owe its citizens?

More government or less government?

Again, because it is so difficult to lay aside our assumptions, before even reading this next section you already have a bias regarding whether or not you want more or less government. But you will learn more in this section if you can lay that aside and really look at both options.

There are many types of governmental rule. Each has its advantages and disadvantages. There is no governmental rule (anarchy); rule by a singular monarch (monarchy); rule by the people (democracy); rule by a small, privileged class (aristocracy); rule by the wealthy (plutocracy); rule by religious leaders (theocracy); rule by military leaders (stratocracy); rule by a dictator (despotism); and many more! Within these systems you have more or less governmental involvement.

Technically, we could say that the smallest government is no government at all. This would be the system of anarchy. However, there are so few people who support anarchy as a serious political position (and its problems are so numerous) that we won't address it here. On the other end of the spectrum would be a government so powerful that all the people in that nation were just slaves without any rights at all. This would happen only in some type of dictatorial monarchy that could literally murder or rape anyone they wanted without penalty. Again, this is not a seriously considered system of government in the modern era. We will therefore rightfully exclude it as well. Within these bizarre extremes of no government and only government, there are a smattering of other positions that allow for more or less government. It is to these positions that we will now turn.

On one end of the spectrum are those who want the smallest government with the least amount of power. The benefit of this system is that it prevents government overreach and maximizes individual liberty. You don't get the socialism of the Nazis or the communism of Stalin when the government stays small and power is in the hands of private citizens. This system maximizes one's individual liberty. Thomas Jefferson's famous dictum about the best government being the one that governs least comes about due to the desire to maximize human freedom apart from governmental interference. Perhaps this is the system with which your sympathies lie. However, even those on this end of the political spectrum usually want some governmental structure. We like the fact that a person cannot raise their own army or own a nuclear weapon. We like driving on public roads and often think that monopolies are bad for capitalism. We think there should be child labor laws, and we call the police when someone is attacking us. We like that CPS can take a child away from a father who puts out cigarettes on them. We also like that our doctors and surgeons have to be qualified by a medical board. And even someone as libertarian as Ron Swanson from *Parks and Rec*[34] can look at statistical data to see that forbidding things like cocaine and prostitution is a great benefit to society.

Who, in a system of minimal government, would take care of the most vulnerable in society? Again, you might say no one, but that doesn't really solve the issue. Do you just allow homeless people to die? Do you allow homeless people any access to medical care, food, or shelter? Perhaps you say, "I wouldn't help the homeless people at all; if they want a better life then they should work harder." Fair enough, *but what if the issue is not just linked to one's ability to work*? What should be done with people who are born with mental disabilities? What should be done with orphans who have nothing and no one to care for them due to no fault of their own? What should be done with people who lost their job due to a recession (who are working their butt off to try to find a new one) and just don't have money to pay for a medical procedure that their child needs to survive?

One may be inclined to say that the government should have absolutely no involvement in one's life or property, but consider this scenario: What if someone owned all the land on which food is grown in a small country and decided that they would not sell it or give it to anyone else? Do these landowners have a right to sentence their fellow citizens to starvation? Does the government have a right to step in and demand that this needed good be sold? Or, if someone invented a cure for cancer, does that person have a right to keep it to themselves and not share the information with anyone else? Or, should the government have the right to step in and save millions of lives? When it comes to basic needs, we all realize that there are certain goods to which everyone should have some access.

On the other end of the spectrum are those who think that the government should have a lot of power and do a lot of decision-making. After all, perhaps if the government could oversee every part of the economy and the means of production, they could make sure that the gap between the rich and the poor was a little less broad. Or, as in communism, they could literally own all the property. This seems to have some advantages in that it would allow people a more level playing field. People would have access to education, medical care, and other things they might not typically receive. It may also promote other community values (other than simply trying to make as much money as you can).

But with material equality, does high governmental intervention cause standards to go down? Does universal education make education standards drop? If everyone has a college degree, then a college degree doesn't mean anything anymore. The academic bar has to be lowered to get enough people over it. And what happens to medical care if doctors can't make as much money as they could without government intervention? Will they work and study as hard? Do you want 60 percent of your income mandatorily going to taxes to pay for someone's voluntary plastic surgery if you work hard and are healthy? How is that fair?

The view that we should have more government has disadvantages, just like the view that we should have less government has disadvantages, the primary objection being that high taxation and positive "rights" hinder progress. If I don't have the ability to keep what I make, what incentive do I have to work hard and grow the economy?

Consider this scenario: Imagine that a teacher told all of her students that, no matter how hard they worked, they would all get a C in the class. The good students, who stayed up late studying, would get a C, and the bad students, who slept through class and never opened a textbook, would also get a C. One may be inclined to say that would be a good thing. After all, in this system nobody would get an F. The "gap" between the rich (A students) and the poor (F students) would certainly be narrowed if everyone got a C. And, noboby would fail.

But would that be best overall? *By making sure that nobody failed, you would also be making sure that nobody really succeeded.* It's not the case that in this system the A students will say, "I'm going to work hard so some of my grade points can go toward the less intelligent students." Rather, they are going to say, "If I have to get a C no matter how hard I work, I won't work at all or I won't put forward my best efforts, because I'll just get a C anyway." The bad students won't say, "Now that I know that I'll get a C instead of an F, I'm going to do my best to study." Rather, they will say, "Since someone else is earning my grades for me, I'm just going to sit back and relax."

In this system, the entire class is brought down. It's not the case that the entire class is brought up. This is why, though varying degrees of socialism are alive and well, *communism* (the maximal view of modern government) as a system has never really worked. Yes, Communists complain that the only reason the system doesn't work is because it has never been implemented rightly. But that is because it *cannot* be implemented rightly. It is based on a logical fallacy. *In true communism, the people should own all the goods equally. In reality, however, only government officials get to own all the goods.* The government takes on the role of the people by proxy, but that is not the same as the individual people actually owning all the goods. The true bourgeoisie become the governmental rulers at the top.

Marxism failed to show itself a good theory for several reasons: (1) as just mentioned, the proletariat, in a communist system, never actually owns the goods—the government does; (2) capitalism was making everyone richer (not just the bourgeoisie); (3) there was a growing and content middle class; (4) the communist revolution didn't happen in the most capitalistic nations as Marx's theory said it logically must; (5) laborers could actually afford their labor (Henry Ford's assembly line workers were paid enough to actually buy the Model T); (6) it was based on a view of humanity that saw us as primarily selfless instead of primarily selfish; and (7) the redistribution of wealth never stays that way as the years go on. This last point is very important to note. Wealth can only ever be distributed equally if you redistribute it every couple of years.

Let's say we did a complete redistribution of wealth. Let's say we took all the money and property in the US and gave everyone an equal share. Would everyone still have the same money and land ten years from then? No. Some people would use their resources wisely, and some people would use their resources unwisely. Economically speaking, *the problem is often a people issue, not a distribution issue.*

You may object and say, "We don't need to redistribute wealth; rather, we need to find a way where everyone has the same starting point." After all, if everyone had the same advantages, then everyone could achieve the same things. But that is just another way of saying that we should redistribute wealth. If a rich kid's parents can hire a tutor and a poor person's parents can't, the only way that they could change this situation is if they were given more money so that they could also hire a tutor. *All attempts to give everyone the same starting point are just a veiled form of giving everyone the same end point.* Not to mention that people who have equal advantages often perform unequally. We all knew some rich kid in high school who went on to become a doctor, but we also all knew some rich kid in high school who was lazy and now cleans restrooms at a movie theater.

None of this information is to say how much influence I think that the government should or should not have. I've pointed out the flaws with minimal government and maximal government only to show that most of us do not live in one extreme or another. We live somewhere in between two extremes.

With minimal government on the one side and maximal government on the other, most people fall into a spectrum involving some view of capitalism or socialism. What is your view on how much control the government should have, and why? This issue seems really complicated, but it usually comes down to what we think is the most important issue: individualism or communitarianism. Is the highest value individual liberty or something else (such as social cohesion, material equality, or other community values)?

Individual freedom or communal good?

Which is more important: what is best for individual liberty (even if it conflicts with what's best for society at large) or what is best for society at large (even if it conflicts with individual liberty)? Is this even a fair dichotomy? What if individual liberty is what's best for society at large? What if communal good is what's best for individual liberty? But for the sake of argument, let's evaluate both sides of the issue.

Let's start with the first option. If you say that individual liberty is the most important value, are there no situations where we might give up some of our liberties for a greater overall good? We have a tendency to think that things such as a public police force are good, but it technically comes at the expense of individual liberty. One would have more freedom to do what they want (and more money to do what they want) if their taxes didn't go to a police force and if they didn't have to follow laws. But, on the other hand, though we hate getting pulled over for speeding, we like the fact that police officers keep us safe from murderers, rapists, and drug dealers who would otherwise ruin society. Individual liberty is definitely a good thing. It is a value that both the left and the right accept. The question comes down to how far this liberty should extend.

In contradistinction to this, perhaps you like the second option: you don't think that personal liberty is the most important value. Perhaps you think the more important value is what is best for society at large, even if it infringes on someone's individual rights. That view runs into quite a few problems as well. *For example, if you hold that what's best for culture at large is more important than individual freedom (in every case), then you have implicitly affirmed slavery.* In slavery, a majority culture of a society benefits greatly because there is an entire workforce that can produce food, build buildings, clean, and do menial tasks. If someone's individual liberty can be taken away as long as it is what is "best" for society at large, then we run into this problem. In fact, many authors in the Greco-Roman world held that slavery was good because it allowed the rest of society to flourish. You cannot have art, music, literature, philosophy, and a well-trained military if everyone has to work to provide their own food.

Most of us, myself included, would say that slavery is a horrendous abuse of human rights. Taking away all of someone's freedom, even if it greatly benefits the community at large, is too high a price to pay for what is best for the culture around us. So perhaps, even if you think what is best for the group should overshadow what is best for the individual, you also agree that there must be limits. *There should be certain rights (speech, religion, etc.) that should not be infringed upon even if we think it would lead to a more successful society.*

As mentioned a couple paragraphs up, some philosophers have pointed out the fact that this bifurcation of individual freedom versus communal good is actually a false dichotomy. *Perhaps individual liberty is also what is best for the community.* Yes, this means that some individuals will have more and others will have less. Yes, this means that there will be a gap between the "haves" and the "have-nots." But perhaps protecting one's rights will lead to the greatest good for the community. By maximizing freedom, one is allowing people to do what they want, pursue business ventures, set up nonprofits, and do many things that benefit the community. Perhaps what is best for the individual is what is best for the community as well.

Conversely, perhaps what is best for the community is what is best for the individual. Yes, this means that some people will have fewer rights and it means that elite performers will be penalized, but it also allows the "have-nots" to have more, it puts everyone on a more level playing field, and it prevents individual interest from being the primary target.

When it comes to the question "Do you think there should be more government or less government?," on what side of the spectrum did you fall before reading this section? Has your view changed at all? If so, why? If not, why not? Regardless of which view you hold, can you list the flaws with your position? Is individual liberty what is best for society at large, or are communal goods what is best for individuals? Are these two ideas in conflict? If so, which should win? If not, why do they seem to conflict on so many issues?

The social contract

When discussing political philosophy, the concept of a social contract often arises. *The social contract is the idea that humans formed government because we thought that the benefits of giving up some of the ability to "do what we want" was worth the safety and protection of having a uniform set of laws and people to enforce those laws.* When discussing a social contract, philosophers are not necessarily saying that there was a time where ancient tribes got together and created an official document written on animal hides. Rather, the idea of a social contract is more of a thought experiment to discuss the origin of systems of justice. It explains how governments might have developed, but it is not essential to the contract's theory whether or not it actually happened. The view of humanity before government is called the *state of nature*, and it tries to imagine what life would have been like before the institutional and codified justice we have today. What would life have been like in this state of nature when there were no laws and everyone did what they wanted?

This all sounds a bit abstract, so let's use an illustration to see this concept more clearly. Imagine that you are part of a very small family of ancient humans a very long time ago. You don't have a written language. You don't have any system of government. You are part of a small band of hunter-gatherers. Life consists mainly of looking for food and trying to mate. Life in this society would probably be pretty terrifying. Life would be, as Thomas Hobbes once quipped, "Nasty, brutish, and short." At any point you could be murdered in your sleep, and there would be no consequences for your killer. At any point you could have your wife taken from you by a man who was stronger (or a better fighter) than you. At any point you could be raped. In this world, every human would have to be on guard against every other human. It would be a war of all against all. If you left to go hunting, someone could come in and steal the berries you collected the day before. If you ran into another band of hunter-gatherers that was bigger than yours, then they could kill you and take all of your belongings. In a society where there was no government at all, there would be only fear and a type of limited anarchy. Anyone at anytime could slit your throat while you were sleeping. You would have to sleep with one eye open and constantly be looking over your shoulder. To get a picture of what this might be like, imagine for a second that the government was dissolved tomorrow. Everyone would break into everyone else's homes and businesses. People would murder those they hate. Some men would rape any woman they could get their hands on. It would be like the movie *The Purge*.[35]

According to Thomas Hobbes, this is exactly what life was like in the state of nature. But, most of us would agree, this would be a terrible way to live. In a sense, this way of life contains maximum liberty—one can even rape and murder as long as they are strong enough to get away with it—but the cost to the quality of life is too great. It allows so much freedom that one can take away the freedoms of others.

In creating a "social contract," what humans decided to do is to formulate laws and appoint sovereigns for the good of human flourishing. Humans decided to bond together to create laws and punishments that everyone must abide by. It is true that humans had to give up some liberty to do this. In a sense a man gives up his "right" to murder so that he is protected from another man's "right" to murder him. Everyone gives up some of the things they might want to do so that they will be protected from another's desires that could be detrimental to them. A modern example of the social contract is the fact that we have speed limits. We are not allowed to drive as fast as we want (which seems like a bummer) until we realize that the speed limit minimizes the chance of someone slamming into us going 150 mph. In short, the social contract is an implicit agreement that there are certain things we should give up, including the freedom to not be under laws, because it leads to a greater overall good than allowing people to do literally whatever they want.

Jean-Jacques Rousseau was a philosopher who also wrote a lot about the social contract, but his view of ancient humanity was the opposite of Hobbes. Whereas Hobbes was very pessimistic about what humans would do without laws and a ruler, Rousseau was very optimistic. For Rousseau, mankind was better back when we were in a state of nature. He believed that humans, before modern society, would have been kind to one another. Humans would have shared their goods with one another. Humans in the state of nature were true to themselves. People lived in a state of harmonious blissfulness. For Rousseau, what actually made culture go awry was the fact that humans began growing society in a way that enshrined institutions. Institutions are things such as religion, family, tradition, government, history, a shared culture, etc. that alienate people who don't fit into the institution's definitions of what one is expected to be. This causes people to be "fake" to try to fit in with larger society; it causes ambition, greed, alienation, and avarice. Rousseau was the great anti-Enlightenment thinker. Whereas everyone else thought institutions were making things better, he thought they made things worse. One can see that his views of the state of nature and the social contract are quite a bit different from Hobbes's.

For Hobbes, the state of nature was bad. For Rousseau, the state of nature was good. For Hobbes, freedom was individual. For Rousseau, freedom was what conformed to the "general will" (which means what the majority in society should want in attempting to dissolve greedy institutions and modern, enlightened society).

As you may have already guessed, if you've read the book this far, ideas have consequences. *"The Terror" during the French Revolution and Marx's system of communism were both explicitly and literally based on Rousseau's theories.*

In the contrast between Hobbes and Rousseau, one thing you will notice is that one's view of human nature directly plays into one's politics. If you think that humans were naturally kind and good in a state of nature, then you will think that the problems in politics are related to things other than human nature. You will want bigger government (because the government will help people). When there is a shooting, you will think the problem is the gun and not the person (because you believe people are naturally good). When someone is sexist or racist, you will think the problem is that the person didn't have the education or upbringing that could have protected them from these vices. But if you think that humans were naturally selfish and bad in a state of nature, you will think that the problems in politics are primarily related to human nature. You will want a smaller government (because you don't trust people in power). When there is a shooting, you will think the problem is the person and not the gun, because a gun doesn't shoot up a mall by itself. When someone is sexist or racist, you will think the problem is that the person is evil, so even if they had had a different upbringing, they could still have chosen to be sexist or racist.

Your political views are not just related to what you read on the news. Your political views are the logical outcome of your . . . wait for it . . . philosophy! Things as abstract as whether or not you believe that people are naturally good or evil will lead you to think certain things about taxation, the legality of marijuana, and LGBTQ+ issues. As I've said throughout the book, philosophy is the foundation for everything else you think you believe. If you get that right, you'll get other issues right. If you get that wrong, you'll get other issues wrong.

Are humans naturally good or bad? Are we naturally selfish or selfless? How does your view accord with Darwinian evolution (meaning, would people have evolved to be self-preserving or to help others primarily)? If you think people are naturally good, why do you have to teach kids what is right but not what is wrong (they already know how to do that)? If we are naturally bad, then why do some people give up their lives to save total strangers?

Miscellaneous categories

Political philosophy is such an enormous subject that we cannot get into every possible detail here. In this last section, we will simply examine some questions related to justice for you to consider in more detail.

What should we think about identity politics? In the traditional view of a classical, liberal, democratic state, people have the right to vote. However, many would say they should use their vote to enact leaders and policies who will do what is best for everyone. *In identity politics, one does not make political decisions based on what is best for everyone. Additionally, one does not make political decisions based on some ideological principle that stands over everyone equally. Rather, in identity politics, one makes political decisions based on a singular goal of a singular group with which they identify.* This group could be based on race, gender, sexual orientation, religion, or a host of other topics. Voters who believe in identity politics are typically one-issue voters. They do not look at all the issues and how all the issues affect everyone. Rather, they focus on some issues much more than others and primarily focus on what is best for their group, even if it is not what is best for other groups.

Should we exalt one political topic above all others (such as morality with regard to religious groups or race with regard to black voters), or should one look for a candidate who values the views of the voters on a host of important issues?

Identity politics was critiqued by Plato long ago. He believed that the worst form of government (other than having a tyrant) was democracy. That sounds insane to us, but his reasoning was partially based on his cultural environment. Where he lived, the largest group of people were the uneducated poor. Plato thought that they cannot set aside their bias and ask, "What is best for everyone?" Rather, when someone is starving, they will ask only, "What is best for me?" Plato, like John Adams, knew that the majority could sometimes be oppressive.

What do you think about Plato's view on democracy? What do you think about identity politics? If you like it, how do you keep one group from unfairly taking advantage of another group? If you don't like it, how do you make sure minority groups are heard? Should political decisions be made by the masses or not? Why?

What does the government owe the least well-off members of society, and how should we make sure everyone has their basic needs and rights met? John Rawls, a famous Harvard political philosopher, gave an example to help us think about his issue. He gave a thought experiment about a "veil of ignorance" that didn't allow us to know into what social class we would be born. If you didn't know who your parents were going to be, and you didn't know if you would be born male or female, and you didn't know what race you were going to be, and you didn't know whether you would be smart or athletic or charming, and you didn't know anything about what your life would be like . . . *what would be the necessary "rights" to which you would want to access?*[36]

To say it another way, imagine that there is a pie and six children who want to eat the pie. You are chosen to cut the pie into different slices so each child can pick their slice, *but you don't know the order in which you will get to select your piece of pie.* If you knew you were going first, you might be inclined to cut the pie into one huge slice and a bunch of smaller slices. After all, you got your (big) piece, so who cares if the other kids get smaller pieces? But if you knew you were going last, then you would want the other kids before you to take smaller pieces of pie so that there would be enough for you. But, due to the veil of ignorance, you don't know the order in which you will get to select your piece of the pie. *The only safe bet is to cut the pie into equal shares so that, no matter what order you go in, you are guaranteed a slice.*

Do you agree with Rawls? What does the government owe the least well off in society (if anything), and how do you prevent people from taking too much "pie" from someone else? What exactly does the government owe you? Is it negative rights such as protection, freedom, and liberty, or do they owe you positive rights such as education, healthcare, and retirement funds? Also, is the analogy of a pie even helpful? After all, money is not like a pie. There is not a set amount of money whereby if one person has more then another has less. Money is always growing, because it is simply a symbol for the amount of goods and services in an economy. What does the government owe the poorest of the poor?

Does the government have a right to control what you do if what you do doesn't physically affect anyone else? We've probably all heard of the idea that I have a right to do what I want only insofar as I don't infringe upon your rights. My right to throw a punch ends at where your nose begins. This idea comes from John Stewart Mill, and it basically says that we have liberty, but not liberty to hinder someone else's liberty.[37] But, Mill goes further: Should the government have a right to hinder my freedoms if they are only physically related to me? If I'm not infringing on someone else's right, then what grounds does the government have to tell me what to do? Shouldn't I have the right to commit suicide? Shouldn't I have the right to take drugs? Shouldn't I have a right to be a prostitute (assuming interactions with my clients are consensual)? Shouldn't I have the right to sell my kidney to a person who needs it so that they don't die? All these things are illegal in the

US, but the question Mill would want us to ask is "Why?" It makes sense that we shouldn't kill other people or that we shouldn't sell drugs to kids or that we shouldn't steal a kidney on the black market (because those affect other people). But what if our actions affect only us and don't physically infringe on someone else's freedoms? What say should the government have over our bodies?

Do groups act, or do only individuals within a group act? There is a very powerful stream of thought in modern politics that treats people as part of a group, *despite the fact that all groups are made up of individuals.* Black people, cops, men, women, white people, LGBTQ+, abortion activists, Evangelicals, and a host of other titles are used as a way to classify people. But "black people" would not exist if individual black people didn't exist. "Cops" would not exist as a category if there were no individual police officers. "Women" would not be a group identity if women had never existed. *As philosophers, we must ask if groups can commit acts or if only individuals (who belong to a group) can commit acts.*

Can "black people" as a faceless, impersonal category commit crime, or can only individual black people commit a crime? Can "white people" as a faceless, impersonal category be racist, or can only individual white people be racist? Can all "cops" as a faceless, impersonal category use too much force, or can only individual police officers use too much force? Can "men" as a faceless, impersonal category rape women, or can only individual men rape women?

This is an interesting question because it is much easier to use a stereotype (regardless of your political affiliation) than it is to do the hard work of asking who is really responsible for an action. A woman has never been raped by the generic category of men. (A bodyless category or definition cannot rape.) Rather, they have been raped by individual men who acted unethically. No one has ever been unjustly shot by the cops as a category. (Categories can't fire bullets.) Rather, they have been shot by individual cops. Can a bodiless entity or group apologize to another group, or can only individuals within a group apologize? When we look at questions like this, we realize how practical philosophy is. For if someone thinks a group can act and another person thinks that only individuals within a group can act, the way we will address grievances changes drastically.

Conclusion

Politics is unlike every other category we have addressed (though it is similar to ethics) because it hits at the very core of who we are as human beings.

At the end of the day, humans live together in communities, so how those communities are governed is extremely important. Unfortunately, most people have never stopped to consider these deeper philosophical questions. Perhaps if they had, our nation (and many other nations) would be far less divided.

In this chapter, we have asked the questions behind the individual political issues of which we are probably very passionate. We have asked the big questions such as: "What is equality?" "Are all forms of equality good?" "What is freedom?" "What does the government owe its citizens (positive or negative rights)?" "How big should the government be?" and many others. And, most importantly, we have been reminded that philosophy is incredibly practical.

It is not a stretch to say that the thing that has killed more people than any other event in human history is not war, plague, earthquakes, or famine—it is bad political ideas. The killing of hundreds of millions by evil rulers over time is directly related to the ideas of the political leaders. Athena is powerful. When she is understood, society flourishes. But when she is misunderstood, people are sentenced to the gulags and the gas chambers.

Conclusion

"But he hasn't got anything on," a little child said "Did you ever hear such
innocent prattle?" said its father. And one person whispered to another what
the child had said, "He hasn't anything on. A child says he hasn't anything on."
"But he hasn't got anything on!" the whole town cried out at last. The Emperor
shivered, for he suspected they were right. But he thought, "This procession
has got to go on." So he walked more proudly than ever, as his noblemen held
high the train that wasn't there at all.

—Hans Christian Anderson, *The Emperor's New Clothes*

I REMEMBER HEARING THE story of *The Emperor's New Clothes* as a child.
In this revealing tale (pun intended) there is a king who has what is said to
be the most splendid, the most glorious, the most stunning set of clothes
ever produced. However, there is a slight problem . . . they don't really exist. This marvelous set of clothes, he is told, can be seen by all the best and
brightest—the cultural elites. It is only the most foolish and contemptible
of people who cannot see the divine wardrobe. So, to make sure he gets
enough social media likes, and to make sure he doesn't get cancelled, the
king acts as though he *can* see them. *In an attempt to seem enlightened to the
cultural around him, he suppresses what he knows to be true.*

When the king goes on display in his birthday suit, the people are all
too eager to affirm what everyone else is affirming. With a cultlike desire
to fit in with the crowd, the masses bow the knee to the prevailing cultural

opinion. What is true takes a back seat to what is avant-garde. What is obvious takes a back seat to what is clearly false.

It is a little child who declares that the emperor is naked.

The child has no political axe to grind. The child has no desire to be approved of by the masses. The child has not had enough time to realize that what is socially acceptable is what a horde of insecure sellouts, pining for public approval, says is acceptable. The child states what is obvious. And, more importantly, *he states what is obvious to everyone else.* But the king has already come this far, and admitting that one is wrong is not *en vogue.* Though everyone knows the king is naked, he must double down and act out this charade all the more. After all, who wants to learn that a little child had more wisdom than a great king with all his people?

The reason I love philosophy is because it plays the role of the child in this story.

When the rest of the world has bought into some bizarre ideology, it is philosophy that stops and screams, "You're naked!" Philosophy doesn't buy into the malarkey that those who refuse to think critically are so quick to adopt. Philosophy is all about what is true and how we know it is true. Philosophy doesn't care how much money you have, what race you are, where you grew up, your favorite color, or your religion. Philosophy is an equal-opportunity hater that demands that everyone fess up to the truth, regardless of what the crowds are doing.

Be wise

Philosophy is the love of wisdom. There is a story about wisdom given in the Hebrew Bible about a king named Solomon. In the story God tells Solomon that he is going to bless him and that he may ask for anything he wants. Instead of asking for money or for his enemies to be destroyed or for an incredibly handsome, Jewish beard, he asks for something move valuable. He asks for *wisdom.* God is delighted at his answer because wisdom is not a selfish request. It is something that benefits others. Wisdom is a gift that keeps on giving. It benefits those who have it, and it benefits those influenced by those who have it.

To show the wisdom that Solomon received, there is a follow-up story about two prostitutes who each have a baby. To clarify this story, we will make up names for the prostitutes. We will call one prostitute Roxy and the other one Stella. (These are obviously not their Hebrew names!) In antiquity, babies often slept in the same bed with their mothers, so that it would be easier to nurse. One night, Roxy accidentally rolls over and smothers her baby in her sleep. When she wakes up she sees that her baby has died. Roxy decides that she will switch her dead baby for Stella's live baby. When Stella is still sleeping, Roxy puts her dead baby in bed with Stella and takes Stella's live baby into the bed with her. When Stella wakes up in the morning, behold, there is a dead baby beside her. But she knows that the dead baby is not hers. Mothers know what their babies look like. Stella knows that Roxy has switched the babies and has stolen her live baby in a fit of jealousy.

So, as the story goes, Roxy and Stella bring their case before king Solomon, the philosopher par excellence. Roxy says that the live baby is hers, and Stella says that the live baby is hers. How on earth will Solomon know who the baby's real mother is? Remember, there is no DNA testing back then. These prostitutes don't have husbands who can testify to what their babies look like. And, since both of the women are presumably about the same age and race, the baby looks like it could belong to either one of them. King Solomon, in a story that has become a paragon of wisdom, takes a sword in his hand. He promises that, since both women are claiming that the baby is theirs, he will cut the baby in half and give half to each of them. After all, it is only fair. If we don't know who is telling the truth, then each of them can have same amount of the baby—half. Roxy believes Solomon's suggestion is a great idea. After all, she is jealous that her baby died, and misery loves company. "Cut the baby in half," she cries! But Stella tells the king not to harm the child. Stella says that Roxy can have the baby, since it will save the baby's life. Solomon states that Stella is the true mother, because he knows that the real mother of the baby will care more about the baby's life than Roxy's desire to have her jealousy appeased.

Wisdom has consequences, and not being wise also has consequences. Far from being a "head in the clouds" exercise, philosophy can change the world. We could have better politics, better counseling, better businesses, better courts, better marriages, and a better society if we would question our beliefs and refuse to be satisfied until we got the answers we were looking for.

In his helpful introductory work *The Problems of Philosophy*, Bertrand Russell shows that the history of philosophy is really a repeated, failed attempt to answer the most basic questions that we have. One might initially be discouraged to hear that philosophy doesn't always give us the answers we want (though many philosophers would disagree and say that it has indeed answered those questions). But, assuming that Russell is right, should we then throw philosophy out the window just because there are many mysteries we have yet to solve? Russell's answer is no. *Philosophy has value in that it teaches us how to think. It teaches us the importance of the mind. It stretches us and makes us ask questions in particular ways.*

Perhaps an illustration (not used by Russell) will be important. Pretend that you are a baseball player and you train every day for the upcoming baseball season. You stretch to become more limber. You lift weights. You run. You practice batting, throwing, and catching. You diet to be more in shape. You practice with your team (which causes you to grow in your ability to work with others and to make friends). You study video footage of opposing teams so you can strategize on how to beat them. After all this work, you find out that the season was cancelled. Has your time all been a waste?

The answer is no. You have grown. You have become stronger, faster, and a better baseball player. You have become a better teammate. You have had to think about how you would beat other teams. And at some point in the future, there will be another season in which you may actually get to play. You see? There is a great benefit in training for baseball, even if you don't get to the game.

Perhaps philosophy is like that. Perhaps learning logic, asking questions about reality, not letting someone off the hook when they present a view without evidence, trying to decipher what makes an action moral or immoral, and thinking really hard about something are inherently valuable practices. After all, a mathematician isn't wasting their time just because they can't ever get to infinity. They still learn quite a bit along the way.

As I said at the beginning of the book, no human can fully master philosophy; nobody can fully master Athena. She's too smart. She's too overpowering. She's too intimidating. She refuses to marry you no matter how many times you beg, and plead, and propose. But this doesn't mean that she gives you nothing. Perhaps, in our attempt to court her we've learned a little bit from going on dates, and taking long strolls, and having conversations over a pint in the pub with her. Whereas, when we started, she was just a girl across the room, by the end of this book perhaps she's looked in our direction and given us a wink.

Epilogue: Postmodernism

For the city was doomed when it took in that [wooden] horse, within which
were all the bravest of the Argives waiting to bring death and destruction
on the Trojans. Anon he sang how the sons of the Achaeans issued from the
horse, and sacked the town, breaking out from their ambuscade. He sang how
they overran the city hither and thither and ravaged it.

—Homer, *The Odyssey*

POSTMODERNITY IS ONE OF the most powerful philosophical influences in
our culture. It is not a unified *Weltanschauung* (worldview) or even a unified
school of thought. Rather, it is a smattering of viewpoints that analyzes the
issues in philosophy from a truly novel and unique position. Thinkers such
as Jacques Derrida, Michel Foucault, Jean-François Lyotard, Jean Baudril-
lard, Richard Rorty, Roland Barthes, et al. promote positions that are unlike
everything else we have studied thus far.

Throughout the book, we have taken the law of noncontradiction as
a given assumption. If one makes a propositional sentence, such as "trees
exist," that sentence cannot both be truth and false at the same time (assuming we don't change the meaning of any of our terms). All rigorous thinking
is based on this assumption. After all, if we contradict ourselves at every
turn, it becomes very difficult to make a sustained and intelligent case for
whatever position we hold.

But postmodernism is not like the rest of philosophy; it is a type of anti-philosophy. It is an intellectual Trojan horse. Unlike all the systems of the past (where thinkers built up enormous, brilliant, and coherent systems of thought), postmodernity doesn't care about playing the same game. Whereas Descartes and Locke were like different teams—but both playing the game of soccer—someone like Lyotard is lighting fires under the bleachers during the match.

Throughout this book, I have tried to remain neutral on almost every position: I gave arguments for and against God's existence. I gave arguments for and against empiricism. I gave arguments for and against Kantian ethics. I gave arguments for and against small government. This doesn't mean that I don't hold a position on each of these topics; it means only that I've tried to keep my viewpoints to myself in an attempt to get you to think about the issues on your own. This chapter, which I have placed as the epilogue, is the only place I'll give my unabashed opinion.

It is my contention that postmodernism certainly has a right to be classified as a type of philosophy. After all, philosophy gets to speak on every topic, and that includes whatever is being said in postmodernism. It is also my contention that many postmodernists are intelligent; one may not like what they say, but they are by no means uneducated. *However, it is also my contention that postmodernism doesn't deserve the same respect as the other types of philosophy we have encountered.* Why is that?

Postmodernism doesn't do the hard work of proving, point by point, its positions. Rather, it often shouts and then runs away with its fingers in its ears, so its opponents cannot show the errors of its reasoning.

Real philosophy must be rigorous. Real philosophy cannot be self-contradictory. Real philosophy must be written clearly, so bad arguments can't hide under confusing language. Postmodernism, however, does none of these.

I'm not the only philosopher who feels this way about postmodernism. When Cambridge University was considering giving postmodern philosopher, Jaques Derrida, an honorary degree, scholars from all over the world protested this act, because Derrida was not doing philosophy but rather literary criticism under the guise of philosophy. Though he is an influential thinker, he doesn't develop, point by point, a clear, noncontradictory system as the great philosophers of the past have done.

But perhaps I'm being too hard on the postmodernists. Allow me to describe what postmodernity is, and you can decide if it falls among the great systems of Plato, Kant, Hegel, et al. or if it is a illogical wolf in philosopher's clothing.

What is postmodernism?

Postmodernism is a term that gets thrown around so much that it has begun to lose its meaning. Interestingly, that is exactly what a postmodernist would want. To define postmodernity by saying that it is simply a denial of absolute truth is too naïve. Postmodernity is not just a rejection of foundationalism and correspondence theories of truth. *Rather, it seeks to say that truth itself is a tool of oppression.*

But we are getting ahead of ourselves. Where does postmodernity come from? At the risk of giving a crass oversimplification, it is the reaction to the arid, sterile, and objective views of truth given during the Enlightenment. To the postmodernist, the views of the Enlightenment sought merely to work out truth calculations in a cultural vacuum instead of actually helping those who were the most vulnerable in society. For most of history, the goal of philosophers was to try see the world the way it "really was" (objectively). The problem with this notion is that it ignores the goals, implications, cultural differences, linguistic differences, political maneuvering, social forces, and a host of other subtleties that are often lurking under the surface any time one claims to possess "truth." *To say it another way, there are larger forces at play (behind the scenes) than just the sterile rationality of Western thought.*

In the premodern era, truth was discovered by revelation (God was thought to reveal truth to man) and was supernatural. In the modern era, truth was discovered by human reason (science and philosophy) yet was still rational. In the postmodern era, truth is deconstructed—truth is no longer objective but rather a veiled attempt at oppressing people—and "truth" (if one can even call it that) is nonrational.

In a sense, postmodernism is contemporary culture's judgment on the arrogance of modernity. During the early modern era, many thinkers had an unbridled optimism in what humans could know through reason and science alone. Postmodernism attempts to critique these bastions of knowledge by deconstructing their claims and turning them inside out.

One scholar helpfully defines postmodernism this way:

> When most philosophers use the word "postmodernism" they mean to refer to a movement that developed in France in the 1960s, more precisely called "poststructuralism." ... They have in mind that this movement denies the possibility of objective knowledge of the real world, "univocal" (single or primary) meaning of words and texts, the unity of the human self, the cogency of the distinctions between rational inquiry and political action, literal

and metaphorical meaning, science and art, and even the possibil-
ity of truth itself.[38]

Truth, for the postmodernist, is not something to be discovered in an ivory tower. Rather, we must take into account how the notion of truth has been used to oppress people. *For the postmodernist, all truth is a power play.* It is an attempt to create an in-group and an out-group. The in-group consists of those who believe in some particular truth. This naturally creates an out-group (those who do not agree with this so-called truth), thus creating what the postmodernist calls "oppression." For example, in the Middle Ages, the truth in Europe was Christianity. To be a Christian was to be in the in-group. If you wanted to become powerful or wealthy or marry well, then you had to (at least culturally) subscribe to Christianity. This created an out-group for Muslims and Jews who were constantly oppressed in Christendom. To give another example, a postmodernist would say that the claim that "homosexuality is immoral" is not an actual claim about objective moral truth (objective moral values do not exist under most forms of postmodernism). Rather, it is an attempt to give power to the in-group (straight people) and to ostracize and disempower the out-group (gay people). Postmodernism is more of a rejection than a continuance of intellectual tradition:

> Simply put, they [philosophers who study postmodernity] regard it as rejecting most of the fundamental intellectual pillars of modern Western civilization. They may further associate this rejection with political movements like multiculturalism and feminism, which sometimes regard the rejected notions as the ideology *of a privileged, sexual, ethnic, and economic group, and aim to undermined established educational and political authorities and transfer the power to the previously disenfranchised.*[39]

The categories of oppressor and oppression are at the heart of postmodern theory. This is why several political activists in the US went on record in 2020 publicly proclaiming that *math is racist*. If all of life is viewed through the lens of oppressed and oppressor, then even something as objective as "two plus two equals four" is actually a way to try to disempower people. After all, those who know math (or logic, as logic is mathematical) create an in-group and an out-group.

There is no way to argue with the postmodernist. Since truth itself is what is in question, the attempt to prove an argument using logic or truth is itself just one more attempt by someone who cares about reason (the in-group) to try to take away the voice of the less rational out-group.

This is why I think postmodernism is an anti-philosophy: *to try to hold the correct view is the entire goal of philosophy, but the postmodernist tries to eliminate that very goal.* Yet, ironically, the postmodernist must use objective standards of logic and argument to prove that there are no objective standards of logic and argument. Thus, the postmodernist can often be found sawing off the tree limb on which they are sitting.

What often goes unseen is the goal of the postmodernist. The postmodernist is no modern-day Robin Hood who wants help those in need. Their agenda is much more sinister. By taking away the power of other groups who claim to have the truth, guess who is left with all the power? *The postmodernist.* The postmodern agenda is not to actually take away the power of the corrupt bourgeois (who have traditionally had it) so they can lift up those who are truly in need. The goal is to use this philosophy to place themselves in power. *The great irony is that those who often condemn "power" are doing so with the intent of having more power.* Their goal is to get society to oppress the (previous) oppressor. The goal is not simply to correct injustice. Rather, they seek to use the dead bodies of the disenfranchised as stepping stones so that they might have all the power. They often use the pains experienced by certain, marginalized groups as a way to exalt themselves.

Society and oppression

According to postmodern philosopher Michel Foucault, part of the goal of postmodernism is to emphasize what has traditionally been marginalized. It is to take what is on the "fringe" and put it in the center. Every society has a dominant culture. Most people in China are Chinese. Most people in Russia are Russian. Most people in India speak Hindi. Most people in Victorian England spoke English. Majority cultures are not bad; in fact, they are necessary. *A culture without anything unifying the citizens isn't a culture at all.* But what the postmodernist wants to say is that any time there is a majority culture, then everyone who is not a part of that culture feels excluded. *And simply to feel different is to (somehow) have less value.* Their solution is to begin to create a new culture. This new culture should not accurately describe the viewpoint of most of the people in that society. Rather, it should seek to take what is fringe and make it look just as normal as baseball and apple pie. When you can't win an argument, there is another way to get people to believe your viewpoint; it is by making your view so ubiquitous that people just assume it. They get used to it, and they become numb to how unlike normal life that view really is for most people.

This is also why there is a current desire to deconstruct traditional intuitions (as we saw with our good buddy Rousseau). Traditional institutions create a unity, and the postmodern movement cannot have a true unity or else others are excluded. Why do you see more statues being torn down? Why do you see people saying that America was founded on genocide (not merely "committed" genocide but was philosophically and ideologically "founded on" genocide)? Why has everything from Thanksgiving, to kindergarten, to the Washington Redskins football team become political? Why is there a push to redefine the nuclear family? The answer is simple: they are traditional institutions.

Church, state, family, government, tradition, language, a shared history, etc. are pillars of Western society. But for the postmodernist, they create a metanarrative of truth that is oppressive to those outside of the *hegemony*. The difficulty, of course, is that without foundational institutions a society cannot flourish. *Diversity is a good thing, but it is good only if it is centered around a unity.* Diversity without something to unify it is simply called division. America has people of varying races, socioeconomic backgrounds, religions, and more, but what is meant to unify us are central institutions (the Constitution, the shared value of individual freedom, family, etc.). However, postmodernism cannot have central institutions lest someone be in the "out-group." Paradoxically, the solution results in making everyone feel left out—everyone feels estranged. *The irony is that postmodernism doesn't make someone who is alienated feel accepted; it simply alienates everyone.* If you can't have standard institutions, then everyone becomes part of the out-group. Postmodernism doesn't value everyone's culture; it values only its own culture, which, ironically, isn't the actual culture of any particular person.

This is one of the reasons why removing labels is so important to the postmodern agenda. If one wants to change or eliminate traditional institutions, then one will need a new language to assist in that endeavor. One cannot identify themselves as a "Jewish man who is an American father" because those are all designators that attach a person to traditional institutions. In that descriptor there is a traditional religion, a binary gender, a national identity, and an appeal to a traditional title in a nuclear family. One cannot call themselves a "Hispanic Christian woman who is also a mother." Rather, the postmodernist would prefer that woman be called a Latinx, fundamentalist, gender X, and birthing parent (or parent number two).

Postmodernism assumes that anyone in power is oppressive and that they received that power only through nefarious means. Allow me to give two examples: When you hear a woman claim that she has been sexually assaulted, before you have any of the facts, is your initial inclination to believe her or to think she is lying? Most people will probably say it is to believe her. When you hear that a police officer shot a person of color, is your first inclination to assume that it may have been racially motivated? Many people will assume it was racially motivated. Why is that? It's not because *most* police shootings are illegitimate (statistically, most of them are justified). It's not because women *never* falsely accuse men of sexual assault when sex was actually consensual (which can and does happen). The reason society begins with the assumption that the officer was at fault and the man was at fault in these two examples is because of the subtle influence of postmodernism. *Men and government officials have had traditional roles of power, and therefore we are inclined to begin with a bias against them when there is a question around their actions.* Don't get me wrong; there has been and is still some racism in law enforcement. Don't get me wrong; many women are sexually assaulted by men, and the stories of those women should be heard (and the men punished). My point in giving these two examples is not political. It is to show that, in a postmodern culture, we begin with a prejudice against groups who have been in power even before we have all the data.

If someone is in a traditional position of power (an institution), they by default are assumed to be an oppressor; they are assumed to be the bad guy. What postmodernism teaches is that someone having a position of power is bad in and of itself (unless, of course, it is someone who holds a postmodern worldview—then, being in power is acceptable).

Satirically, the movement doesn't actually attempt to give all marginalized groups power. *It seeks to give power only to groups who can help move forward its political and social agenda.* Intellectual historian Carl Trueman states,

> *Interestingly enough, the "Other" is rarely defined by such post-moderns in terms with which the middle-class intelligentsia would be uncomfortable: members of the Ku Klux Kan, Holocaust deniers, serial killers, and collectors of other people's toenail clippings would all seem to have first-class claims to having been marginalized and written out of the dominant narratives of this world; but none, so far as I know, enjoys the support of a significant postmodern lobby group.*[40]

The movement is not actually about giving a voice to everyone who is marginalized; it is about using marginalized groups to help put the leaders in power.

If you are beginning to notice a pattern, you are not wrong. The movement intentionally seeks to promote crowd control (and to shut down independent thinking), not by making actual arguments for certain positions but by using the opium of repetition and by convincing privileged Westerners that they are the most oppressed group in world history. The goal of postmodernism is to end all objective conversation; the goal is to prevent people from hearing both sides of an argument. If you allow people to hear differing viewpoints, then you are acquiescing to the idea of truth, and the postmodernist cannot have truth. The goal must be to yell louder and to cancel those who disagree with you. If they can use a word or phrase enough times, they can push an ideology through our subconscious without actually having to make a case for its soundness.

Postmodernism in education

In case you can't tell, I am a big proponent of education. Education is the key that unlocks the world. I personally want higher standards (not lower). I personally want more academic rigor (not less). I personally want education to move away from the pragmatic goal of getting a job to make money and move toward the more noble goal of knowing truth through studying the liberal arts. Most philosophers agree with me. *The life of the mind is the best life.* But the postmodernist seeks a different goal in education.

Traditionally, the goal of education was to lay aside one's ignorance and to learn from others. It was not to ask what you, as an ignorant beginning student, thought about something. Rather, you were supposed to be formed by the great minds that came before you. Plato was a greater thinker than you, regardless of his strange views about religion. Aristotle was a greater thinker than you, regardless of his barbaric views about women. Descartes was a greater thinker than you, despite the fact that he didn't have a smartphone and his mustache was too thin.

The goal of education was for you to change. The student's job was not simply to become entrenched in the views they already held. (If that was the goal, then there was no point in going to school in the first place.) Rather, the student was to lay aside the ignorance with which they had begun so that they could be corrected. One entered school as a student and left as a master. In postmodernity, however, the goal is the opposite. Today, a student enters school as a master in that any claim that doesn't already agree with their worldview is jettisoned. They are not taught to understand Aristotle; they are taught to dismiss Aristotle because he believed in slavery. They are not taught to understand Machiavelli; they are taught to dismiss Machiavelli because of his misogynistic language about beating Lady Fortune into submission. They are not taught even to understand American politics; they are taught to dismiss anything that a twenty-first-century American would find offensive today.

The irony, again, is the arrogance in treating education this way. One doesn't learn anything in this system that one doesn't already know. Some nineteen-year-old kid who lives in his mom's basement is treated as more enlightened than Plotinus, Hegel, Nietzsche, or Augustine. Postmodernism is the death of education. *If truth is a way to oppress others, then only the most ignorant will be thought the most intelligent.*

Poststructuralism and language

To understand postmodernism, we must also understand a little bit about how postmodernists view language in what is technically known as *post-structuralism*. And to understand *post*structuralism, we must first understand structuralism. Without getting into the weeds of hermeneutics and linguistic theory, *structuralism is a way of understanding how language has meaning by comparing and contrasting the different meanings of signs and their concepts within a larger linguistic framework.* The major proponent here is the Swiss linguist and philosopher Ferdinand de Saussure. The question Saussure is trying to answer is "What makes words mean what they do?" Or, more simply, how do words mean? Words might get there meaning from a tradition and culture (i.e., Gadamer); or words might have meaning based on how they function in a picture-like logical structure that mirrors reality (i.e., early Wittgenstein); or words might have practical language games whereby we act a certain way in a certain situation by knowing the rules of the game (i.e., later Wittgenstein); or words might get their meaning from the mental picture one has in their mind when they use them (i.e., Augustine); or, as Saussure thought, *words might have meaning based upon how those words contrast and interrelate to other words within a larger linguistic structure and language.*

That sounds very technical, so allow me to simplify. When I want to know what the word *shoe* means, the words with which it interacts (in a larger language structure) are how I come to know the word's meaning. The word *shoe* is linked to words like *foot, laces, sole,* etc. This is structuralism. Someone who is poststructural agrees that words interact with other words; *however, they don't think this actually helps you find truth or meaning; they believe this makes truth impossible.* Instead of signs contrasting and cohering with other signs to get meaning, the poststructuralist believes this puts one into an infinite regress where truth is impossible. To say it more clearly: *when you look up the meaning of a word in a dictionary, you get the definition in the form of other words. You then have to look up the meaning of those words. This creates an infinite regress, so you never get to the true meaning of the word.*

Confused yet? That is structuralism on the linguistic side. But there was another type of structuralism on the anthropological side. Claude Lévi-Strauss promoted the idea that there are certain paradigms that are similar throughout different cultures.[41] Perhaps cultures all share certain notions that are hardwired into us. The differences among societies are small, but they are all based on a larger structure thought to be common to all humans. The postmodernists also disagree with this notion and think that there are no common grids or structures through which different cultures agree on how to view life.

Derrida questioned the ability of language (through which we express all our ideas) to relate objectively to the "real world." He would point out that we can't actually know the "real world" nor accurately express it with our language. We can know only language; we can know only the text. We cannot get beyond the text. Words are, to use his concept, "polysemic" and have a host of meanings related to the varied and multifaceted meanings of other words.[42]

What does all this mean? Let's use an example to break it down. As we just stated, when you want to define a word, how do you do it? Well, you usually look it up in a dictionary. And how does the dictionary define that word? Well, by using other words. And how do you know what those words mean? Well, you have to look them up in another part of the dictionary—*ad infinitum*. You can't get beyond the words. You can't get beyond to text.

This is exactly what Derrida wants. If he can destroy our ability to know objective reality, he can shift the paradigm of philosophy in a radically new direction. This is one of the reasons why he preferred written texts to spoken dialogue. When someone is speaking to you, their ideas are directly related to their intent and to objective meaning (we can ask someone who is speaking what they mean if we misunderstand something they say). Derrida prefers a reader-response theory of hermeneutics whereby one is able to read their meaning onto a text regardless of what the author intended when they wrote it. Every author is a "dead author," and the author's intent is irrelevant. Ideas like Derrida's, if correct, could mean the death of all truth and objective knowledge.

Conclusion

So . . . did I persuade you? Of course, I didn't win over the postmodernist, because all the arguments I just gave were based on logic, and the postmodernist doesn't believe in the historic view of logic. But perhaps that proves the point that I set out to make in the beginning: postmodernism isn't real philosophy—it is anti-philosophy. Many philosophers have pointed out the irony when a postmodernist tries to defend postmodernism. They must appeal to the very method and system of inquiry that they hate. To try to prove that there is no universal, objective truth requires that you appeal to universal, objectively true points to make your argument.

This does not mean that we should not study postmodern philosophy. We must study it. We can learn something from everyone, if nothing else than how to make better arguments. Additionally, we cannot do what the postmoderns do in promoting cancel culture. Everyone should get a chance to fully express their position, without interruption. After all, if you hold a strong enough, logical position you shouldn't feel threatened by someone's opposing viewpoint.

It is mark of an educated mind to be able to hear a position with which you disagree without becoming emotional or upset. With this definition we see that the mind of the general populace often lacks this most essential mark.

Endnotes

1. To my knowledge, medieval scholastics never actually debated this topic (though it is often used as an example of how scrupulous and superficial their questions were). It is actually an excellent philosophical question if you think about it: How does a nonphysical being (such as an angel) relate to physical space?

2. A really helpful anthology for selections of many of the great works of philosophy is Cahn, *Classics of Western Philosophy.*

3. My introductory logic book is called *Logic for Christians: Critical Thinking for the People of God*, which I'd recommend if you want to explore logic from a religious perspective. But since it is written from a religious perspective (and this book is not), if you would prefer one that is more value neutral I'd recommend: McInerney, *Being Logical.*

4. I especially like: Solomon, *Introducing Philosophy*, 9th ed. They have newer editions of this work, but I think this version is better than the newer ones.

5. Whitehead, *Process and Reality*, 39.

6. Aristotle, *Cat.* 5.2a.11–19 (quoted in Kenny, *New History of Western Philosophy*, 102).

7. Wachowskis, *Matrix.*

8. It should be noted here that by the word "God," Spinoza does not mean a personal God such as in Judaism, Christianity, and Islam. His God is more of a ground of being for the universe and not a personal God.

9. Camus, *Myth of Sisyphus*, 19–20.

10. I once heard this in a philosophy lecture but cannot remember where.

11. Bird, "Thomas Kuhn."

12. See Luttrell, *Lone Survivor*.

13. Since Kant wrote in German (and changed his definitions slightly throughout his works) there is no one "official" categorical imperative in English. I have used this one because it is simple. For the other descriptions of the imperative see both *Critique of Practical Reason* and *Groundwork of the Metaphysics of Morals*.

14. Solomon and Higgins, *Big Questions*, 254.

15. Moore, *Knowing Reality*, 293.

16. Hume, *Dialogues Concerning Natural Religion*, 15.

17. Lewis, *Mere Christianity*, 6.

18. Hamilton, *Pirates*, 17.

19. McGrath, *Christian Theology Reader*, 16–17.

20. Anselm, *Proslogion*, 74–75.

21. Descartes, *Meditations on First Philosophy*, 44.

22. Edwards, "Of Being," 9.

23. Kant, *Critique of Pure Reason*, 585.

24. Effington, *Metaphysics*, 163.

25. Calvin, *Institutes of the Christian Religion*, 1:44, 1:46.

26. Sproul, *Classical Apologetics*, 322.

27. This adaptation and extension from Hume was originally an idea from certain Greek thinkers. Quoted here from "Reason 68" in GMSEED, *101 Reasons Why*, 70.

28. Paraphrased from Boethius, *Consolation of Philosophy*, bk. 4.

29. McGrath, *Christian Theology Reader*, 182.

30. This is not one quote but a smattering of quotes from Aquinas about faith and reason taken from *Summa Theologia*. A good resource for Aquinas's view on reason and for quotations around it is Kretzmann and Stump, *Cambridge Companion to Aquinas*.

31. See https://rintintin.colorado.edu/~vancecd/phil201/Searle.pdf.

32. Manson, "Tumbling Ground for Whimsies."

33. Kenny, *New History of Western Philosophy*, 52; cf. Plato, *Resp.* 5.451d–471c.

34. See Daniels and Schur, *Parks and Recreation*.

35. DeMonaco, *Purge*.

36. Rawls, *Theory of Justice*, 136.

37. See Mill, *On Liberty*.

38. Cahoone, *From Modernism to Postmodernism*, 2.

39. Cahoone, *From Modernism to Postmodernism*, 2; emphasis mine.

40. Trueman, *Histories and Fallacies*, 53.

41. See Lévi-Strauss, *Tristes Tropiques* and *Structural Anthropology*.

42. See Derrida, *Of Grammatology*.

Bibliography

Anselm of Canterbury. *Proslogion*. In *A Scholastic Miscellany: Anselm to Ockham*, translated by Eugene R. Fairweather, 69–93. Library of Christian Classics: Ichthus. Philadelphia: Westminster, 1981.

Bird, Alexander. "Thomas Kuhn." *The Stanford Encyclopedia of Philosophy*, Aug. 13, 2004; substantive revision Oct. 31, 2018. https://plato.stanford.edu/entries/thomas-kuhn/#ConcPara.

Cahn, Steven. *Classics of Western Philosophy*. 8th ed. Indianapolis: Hackett, 2021.

Cahoone, Lawrence E. *From Modernism to Postmodernism: An Anthology*. Blackwell Philosophy Anthologies. Oxford: Blackwell, 1996.

Calvin, John. *Institutes of the Christian Religion*. Edited by John T. McNeill. Translated by Ford Lewis Battles. 2 vols. Louisville: Westminster John Knox, 2011.

Camus, Albert. *The Myth of Sisyphus*. Translated by Justin O'Brien. Toronto: Random House, 1955.

Daniels, Greg, and Michael Schur. *Parks and Recreation*. Aired Apr. 9, 2009—Feb. 24, 2015, on NBC.

DeMonaco, James. *The Purge*. Universal City, CA: Universal, 2013.

Derrida, Jacques. *Of Grammatology*. Translated by Gayatri Chakravorty Spivak. Baltimore: Johns Hopkins University Press, 1997.

Descartes, René. *Meditations on First Philosophy*. Translated by Donald Cress. Indianapolis: Hackett, 1993.

Edwards, Jonathan. "Of Being." In *A Jonathan Edwards Reader*, edited by John E. Smith et al., 9–13. New Haven, CT: Yale Nota Bene, 2003.

Effington, Nikk. *Metaphysics: The Key Concepts*. New York: Taylor & Francis, 2010.

GMSEED. *101 Reasons Why God Does Not Exist*. N.p.: n.p., 2019.

Hamilton, Sue. *Pirates: Bartholomew Roberts*. Edina, MN: Abdo, 2007.

Hume, David. *Dialogues Concerning Natural Religion*. 2nd ed. Indianapolis: Hackett, 1998.

Kant, Immanuel. *Critique of Pure Reason*. Translated by Werner Pluhar. Indianapolis: Hackett, 1996.

———. *Groundwork of the Metaphysics of Morals*. Translated by Mary Gregor and Jens Timmermann. 2nd rev. ed. Cambridge Texts in the History of Philosophy. Cambridge: Cambridge University Press, 2012.

Kenny, Anthony. *A New History of Western Philosophy*. 2010. Reprint, Oxford: Oxford University Press, 2012.

Kretzmann, Norman, and Elenore Stump, eds. *The Cambridge Companion to Aquinas.* Cambridge: Cambridge University, 1993.

Lee, Zach. *Logic for Christians: Critical Thinking for the People of God.* Houston: Lucid, 2021.

Lévi-Strauss, Claude. *Structural Anthropology.* Translated by Claire Jacobson and Brooke Grundfest Schoepf. New York: Basic, 1974.

———. *Tristes Tropiques.* Edited by Patrick Wilcken. Translated by John Weightman and Doreen Weightman. London: Penguin, 2012.

Lewis, C. S. *Mere Christianity.* Siloam Springs, AR: Granite, 2006.

Luttrell, Marcus. *Lone Survivor: The Eyewitness Account of Operation Redwing and the Lost Heroes of SEAL Team 10.* New York: Back Bay, 2008.

Manson, Neil. "'A Tumbling Ground for Whimsies'? The History and Contemporary Role of the Conscious/Unconscious Contrast." In *History of the Mind-Body Problem*, edited by Tim Crane and Sarah Patterson, 156–76. London Studies in the History of Philosophy 3. Abingdon: Routledge, 2000.

McGrath, Alister. *The Christian Theology Reader.* 5th ed. Oxford: Wiley-Blackwell, 2016.

McInerney, D. Q. *Being Logical: A Guide to Good Thinking.* New York: Random House, 2004.

Mill, John Stuart. *On Liberty.* Edited by Elizabeth Rapaport. Indianapolis: Hackett, 1978.

Moore, Dwayne. *Knowing Reality: A Guided Introduction to Metaphysics and Epistemology.* Peterborough, Can.: Broadview, 2023.

Rawls, John. *A Theory of Justice.* Cambridge, MA: Harvard University Press, 2005.

Russell, Bertrand. *The Problems of Philosophy.* Portland, OR: Gray Cadence, 2011.

Searle, John. "The Chinese Room." https://rintintin.colorado.edu/~vancecd/phil201/Searle.pdf.

Solomon, Robert. *Introducing Philosophy: A Text with Integrated Readings.* 9th ed. Oxford: Oxford University Press, 2008.

Solomon, Robert, and Kathleen Higgins. *The Big Questions: A Short Introduction to Philosophy.* 8th ed. Belmont: Wadsworth, 2010.

Sproul, R. C. *Classical Apologetics.* Grand Rapids: Zondervan, 1994.

Trueman, Carl. *Histories and Fallacies: Problems Faced in the Writing of History.* Wheaton, IL: Crossway, 2010.

Wachowskis, The. *The Matrix.* Burbank, CA: Warner Bros., 1999.

Whitehead, Alfred North. *Process and Reality: An Essay in Cosmology.* New York: Free Press, 1979.

9 798385 200375